About the Author

Born in Sheffield in 1950, Bill joined the army at the age of fifteen and a half. He joined The Parachute Regiment as a musician and enjoyed many overseas postings, with tours in Northern Ireland, France, Cyprus, Kenya, Iran, Bermuda and the USA. He also attended The Royal Military School of Music, Kneller Hall. He culminated his army career in 1977 as an instructor at the regiment's depot.

Bill is now retired, lives with his wife of fifty-one years, and continues to grapple with his rogue gene.

My Rogue Gene

William A Pollard

My Rogue Gene

Olympia Publishers
London

www.olympiapublishers.com
OLYMPIA PAPERBACK EDITION

A CIP catalogue record for this title is
available from the British Library.

ISBN: 978-1-80074-296-3

This is a work of creative nonfiction.
The events are portrayed to the best of the author's memory.
While stories in the book are true, names and identifying details
have been omitted to protect the identity of the people involved.

First Published in 2022

Olympia Publishers
Tallis House
2 Tallis Street
London
EC4Y 0AB

Printed in Great Britain

Dedication

To Sheila, my wife of fifty-one years.

One of my better choices in life.

She has picked me up and dusted me down on each and every
one of my life's collisions.

Never complaining. Always contented.

There aren't many like her around!

Bill's Prologue

 I've got this rogue gene.

I haven't given it a name… Well, I have, but I don't want to offend any delicate sensitivities at this early stage.

Generally, you know, I've had a good life. I've had lots of laughs, I've had some really good friends, I've done some amazing things and I'm proud of what I've achieved in the years I've taken up a tiny space on this planet. My biggest achievement is being married to the same wife for fifty-one years!

Unfortunately, my rogue gene has done everything possible to make my life challenging, to say the least. It sits there, in the folds of my scrotum, just waiting to pounce. On numerous occasions, when I've tried to do something good or when I'm feeling happy with my labours, this bloody rogue gene insists on… Well, complicating things. You'll see. I can't do anything about it 'cos I was born with it, but I'm confident that many other people around the world possess a rogue gene similar to mine and they'll know exactly what I've had to contend with.

But let's not dwell on my rogue gene yet. Let's take a look at me.

I was born in Sheffield, Yorkshire. Not many people know this, but Yorkshire is the centre of the Universe.

At the time of writing, I am almost seventy-one years old. For those of you that are useless at maths, like me, I'll help you out by confirming that I was born on the thirteenth of May, 1950. Luckily, that day was a Saturday so I just missed being born on unlucky Friday the 13th. But that didn't count for anything. My rogue gene has never cared what day I was born on. According to the rhyme, 'Saturday's child works hard for a living'. My rogue gene has certainly made sure of that!

And another thing, with age comes a label that describes me, and many others perfectly. A grumpy old man!

I could cut and paste my curriculum vitae for you, but I'm not going to. Those things are boring and, in my opinion, mostly fabrications to try to persuade a prospective employer that you are better than you actually are. You don't want to work for any employer that is fooled by a CV. He really must be a fool if he relies on an exaggerated narrative to decide whether you've got the job! CVs are also a method of boosting someone's ego, so I'm not going to regurgitate mine. I've done that on several occasions when my rogue gene has expedited a change in my career.

Throughout my life I've been to lots of places and done lots of things in those places. To quote a phrase, "I've got about ten t-shirts". Consequently, I have accrued lots of stories about my escapades. However, these are all in my memories. I've never written them down, but I have, on various occasions, related some yarns for the entertainment of my family (usually my grandchildren) and friends.

After each rumination I am told the same thing, "You should write that down." Now I've heard this mantra a lot but I've never done anything about it. However, there are several events, recently, that have provided the time for me to think about my past and fulfil the task suggested to me.

The first is the fact that I'm now retired. In fact, I retired in 2005 just after my fifty-fifth birthday. I took early retirement because I'd had enough of walking about on the bottom of somebody else's shoe and, most importantly, my wife continued to work. Her choice.

Now, retiring early doesn't necessarily mean that I have loads of time. I don't. In fact, there's a lot of truth in the old adage, "Now I've retired I've never been so busy". I'm a published composer and I have filled my time by composing and arranging music for concert bands, singers and local music groups. I'm also the founding member of my town's own concert band. Even so, my rogue gene has prevented me from becoming famous except, perhaps, in my own mind.

The second event that has enabled me to ruminate on my past is that right now, 2021, a most malicious and highly contagious virus (Covid-19) has descended on us, forcing the government to impose a lockdown on virtually every person and business in the UK. At the time of writing, we are unable to leave our homes to meet other people in fear of spreading this insidious disease any more widely than it already is, although the lockdown restrictions do change occasionally, generally adding confusion to our lives.

I've had this virus and it's not nice, probably enticed upon me by my rogue gene. I was in our local theatre enjoying a film put on for senior citizens and behind me sat a woman who constantly coughed onto the back of my neck. The film finished and we all trooped towards the exit. I found that the back of my head was, literally, wet! It's true. It seems my rogue gene fancied a shower. I'm convinced that's how the virus was passed on to me.

A third reason to relate my escapades to the world at large is that my memory is, inevitably, beginning to fade. My wife is getting a little fractious at having to watch a film that, "I'm sure I've never seen before." Although with a fading memory watching a film for a second, or even third time, is equally as enjoyable as the first viewing!

So, I thought it about time that I let people know that you are not alone if your rogue gene is making life difficult for you. Some would say it's bad luck, but believe me, nobody, and I mean nobody, can have as much bad luck as I've had without having a rogue gene lurking somewhere personal, just waiting to pounce.

I've enhanced many of my adventures with disguises to make the events more... What shall we say? Interesting? I might even have added a few urban myths.

Some of you might read this book and say, "That's bullshit," or, "That didn't happen like that," or "What a load of bollocks." I don't care!

Are the events described in these tales real? Did they really happen? You must decide what is the truth and what is pure fiction.

I'm not going to mention any names. Some of the people cited have probably died by now, anyway. That's their problem. However, when I describe an incident involving others, if you are still alive you will know who you are, who was involved and what actually happened.

And another thing. Be warned! Political correctness was not a term recognised back in the days I'm about to recall. In those days there was no political correctness. None. Black was black and white was white. Blokes were "blokes" and women were "birds". Fat people were, well... Fat. Don't, therefore, be offended if I make a politically incorrect remark. It's the way things were in those days. Anyway, if you are offended, I don't care! Okay?

Now, in anticipation of actually getting this book published, I'll make the following statement:

"Characters, businesses, places, events and incidents could be the product of the author's imagination or might be used in a purely fictitious manner. Any resemblance to actual persons, living or dead, or actual events, may be purely coincidental."

So, my book is about me. I wouldn't exactly call it an accurate autobiography. It's more a spoof of my autobiography covering just my childhood and army life, a period of twenty-seven years.

But there is a small element of truth somewhere in the text... Isn't there?

BOOK 1
YOUNG BILL

CHAPTER 1
Bill's Rogue Gene.

My mum with my peers at Holgate Avenue. I'm on the far left.

I don't know where my rogue gene came from. I can only guess.

All I know is that this evil, malevolent, spiteful, nasty, vicious, revolting, nauseating, antagonistic, and ugly, creature resides in me. Inside me! In the folds of my ballbag specifically. That's where it hides.

You'll gather that this thing is no friend of mine. In fact, I hate it. The damage it's done to me is enough to make anyone swear!

I can only assume that it lives inside my ballbag because it's logical that I've inherited it from one of my ancestors. I've got no real proof that any of my ancestors had a hand in creating the little sod but I must have been born with it 'cos you can't assemble one of these things then magically transfer it into your being. It has to be inherited. And if it is inherited it must have originated from some other bloke's ballbag because that's how you inherit genes, isn't it? But which of my forefathers passed it down the line to me?

I've wondered about this for years. Ever since my school days. That's when I began to realise that my destiny was being influenced by something sinister and annoying. Something that I have had no control over.

In recent years I've dabbled in the pastime of constructing one's family tree. Now, I know that I'm not going to find the specific identity of the originator of this obnoxious creature, but I might get some idea of the time my own rogue gene's ancestor got launched into some unsuspecting female. My research has uncovered several possibilities.

The earliest time I have been able to research my ancestral line is back to 1660. In those days my ancestral fathers had names like Franciscam, or Malachi. That was their problem. However, the prime suspect is my great, great granddad (1835 - 1906). By all accounts he seemed normal, but could he have been the catalyst that sparked a new line in Pollard problems? I suppose one of his ancestors might have nurtured a distant rogue gene within their reproductive organs, but some signs point to him.

He had a single child, a daughter (1862 – 1938), my great grandma. Nothing wrong with that. Lots of couples had daughters at that time, but did he manufacture a rogue gene in her for onwards transmission? Who knows?

The problem with this particular daughter was that although she got married twice, there is absolutely no evidence that she was married at the time that she gave birth to my granddad. So granddad (1881 – 1952) may well have been born out of wedlock. Bad girl! Did he who made her pregnant, the randy scoundrel, the cad, by any chance pass on a rogue gene to be inherited by my granddad? Who knows? Maybe he was a psychopath. Maybe he was a serial shagger, a creator of illegitimate children. Who knows?

My other suspect is my great, great, great granddad (1811
– 1857). Now he had a lot of bad karma. For a start, nobody
can find his parents. I've approached a professional
genealogist to search for them, but even she could find no trace
of my great, great, great granddad's background. Maybe one
of his ancestors passed on the rogue gene. Who knows? But
the most pertinent clue to his rogue gene is the fact that at the
age of forty-six, young by all accounts, he died in a coal
mining accident at Lundhill Colliery, near Barnsley.

It's bad enough that he had to work in an environment
guaranteed to make him ill with the terrible, debilitating
diseases pneumoconiosis, also known as miner's lung, black
lung disease or just black lung. But on the 19th February, 1857,
at approximately twelve twenty p.m. a huge explosion, caused
by the mixture of airborne coal dust and oxygen, killed two
hundred men and boys aged between ten and fifty-nine years.
The explosion was so powerful that one of the cages was
blown up and out of shaft two. A prodigious amount of smoke,
dust and fire ascended from shaft three and was visible from
miles away. Great, great, great granddad and his brother were
two of those killed as they ate their lunch. Ironically, twenty-
two men had decided to return to the pit head to eat their lunch.
Maybe they didn't have a rogue gene. I'm pretty convinced
that great, great, great granddad did, and maybe it was passed
to my great, great granddad. Who knows?

So, there you go. Two very valid reasons for me to suspect
that a rogue gene has been bestowed upon me.

My heart goes out to anyone that recognises and accepts
that they are endowed with the rogue gene syndrome. There is
no cure. There is no vaccine, or pill, or inhaler, or even

operation to repair this affliction.

You just have to live with it…

CHAPTER 2
Bill Stacking Bin Lids

I was born in Sheffield, Yorkshire. You know that Yorkshire is the centre of the universe, don't you?

Anyway, I knew from the moment I was born that I had inherited a rogue gene 'cos the nurse dropped me as soon as I entered the world. I suppose I must have been exceedingly slippery from all the gunge that got expelled from my mum's womb, but fortunately I landed on the bed between Mum's legs. A soft, but nonetheless an unpredicted and startling landing.

"Everything's OK," they said, to mum's relief. Everything was definitely not okay. I'm sure I heard some laughter. Maybe that was from the nursing staff but I'm now convinced, seventy years on, that it was from my rogue gene, enjoying the moment.

I was carried by Mum to my first home in Holgate Avenue, Sheffield. We went on the bus. I vaguely recollect that the homes were small terraced two storey houses with a tunnelled access dividing alternate abodes. The tunnel between the homes led to the back gardens of the two adjacent homes, with a brick outside toilet block at the end of the tunnel accommodating a single toilet pan and small storage shed adjacent to each of the homes.

The toilet block gave me my first insight to rogue genes because one of my earliest memories is of watching my dad's boots disappearing through the toilet window to rescue our neighbour's young daughter. She had got herself locked in the toilet and her screaming alerted everyone from about two miles out. Dad emerged with a bloody nose and black eye. His hand had slipped on the edge of the toilet pan and he nose-dived onto it. It all falls into place now... My dad had a rogue gene and he passed it onto me!

My family then moved to a place called Hackenthorpe, a council estate on the outskirts of the city. This place is surrounded by estates with typical Yorkshire names; Frecheville, Intake, Birley, Woodhouse, Owlthorpe and Beighton. These are my stomping grounds and places where I've had many adventures.

I grew up with three brothers, two of them older than me, and an older sister. She was the eldest of my peers. The eldest of my brothers was tall, built like a towering office block. Really tall. If he was alive now, I would have one thing to say to him, "You are tall!" He was the leader of our 'gang', and with my other elder brother we were 'The Untouchables' of Hackenthorpe. We got up to all sorts of fun (trouble). None of the other kids on the estate would bother us because my two older brothers would "see to them" if they did. At that time, I guess I was about ten or eleven years old, and during the weekend and school holidays we three disappeared from home all day. Sometimes into the night.

In the balmy summer evenings, we occasionally played a game called 'Stacking Bin Lids'.

The houses on our estate, generally, were semi-detached and all the entrance doors faced each other across a shared path. The doors opened inwards and each door had an integral letter box and door knocker. The door knocker was an extremely useful implement... Not just for knocking on doors.

We got some string out of Dad's shed and when nightfall descended on us we would go to a part of the estate that we knew Mum or Dad never went and we would pick an unsuspecting house to victimise. Quietly, one of us would lift the dustbin lid off its base and tie one end of the string to its handle, situated on the top of the lid. We then carefully tied the other end of the string to the door knocker, thereby suspending the bin lid against the door. The next task was to collect as many empty [glass] milk bottles from the surrounding houses and stack as many as we could on top of the dustbin lid. This whole exercise was well planned, with each one of us delegated by my eldest brother to complete one of the tasks without making any noise — remove the bin lid, tie the string and collect the bottles. If we made any noise, you could bet your trousers that someone would poke their face through the drawn curtains and most certainly raise the alarm.

Having completed phase one of the exercise, phase two was easy. You rap on the door and leg it!

The fun wasn't so much in watching what happened, we couldn't 'cos we were legging it... It was the thought of the door being opened by Mr. or Mrs. Householder who sees this bin lid swing inwards and wallop the door frame, followed by the audible crash of smashing milk bottles on the concrete porch step as the bottles got knocked off the bin lid. Inevitably, the then famous phrase, "You bloody nuisance. If I get hold of you, you'll bloody well suffer!" would be bellowed across the estate in our direction. Sometimes the message was varied… "I know who you are and I'll tell your dad!" But we didn't stop running and we didn't stop laughing for ages.

Sometimes, we would vary our strategy.

Instead of stacking bin lids we would merely tie the opposing door knockers together, tightly, then rap on both doors. All we needed to do then was to stand on the path and watch as two testosterone filled angry bulls tried to open their doors. There was always much heaving from both sides and the sounds of a great deal of choice words swelled into a frenzied roar from both quarters. Oh boy! Usually the male occupants got angry, and the verbal abuse got more vociferous and more colourful as they heaved on their doors to open them.

We didn't need to leg it immediately because we knew the occupants of both houses were effectively tied inside. We did, however, have to keep an eye on the front windows because that was the preferred egress point to find out, "What the bloody hell is going on?" As soon as we saw a raging animal coming out of the window, feet first and turning the air blue with choice threats, we were off. The fastest sprinters on the estate.

At school, the next day we inevitably had a lecture from the headmaster during assembly about the consequences of being caught doing these "acts of stupidity". My brothers and I couldn't help but chuckle from our downturned heads as we pictured the previous night's experience.

Now, I hear you ask, "What did your rogue gene do to spoil this fun?"

Well, it didn't spoil my fun all the time but on occasion

one of us was caught. Usually me 'cos I was the smallest and also the slowest runner. Sometimes we were recognised and informed on to our dad.

One of two things would happen if one of us was caught. Either the guy, it was usually the man of the house, would give he who was caught a good hiding and told to, "Get home and tell your dad what I've done." We never did, or we would be physically carried home for our dad to give us a good hiding.

Dad knew absolutely everybody on the estate and he didn't need to be told what we had done. It was, "Our Billy again? I'll see to it," and I was handed over for my punishment.

On one occasion I got two hidings.

I was caught by our local police sergeant while me and my brothers were stacking bin lids. Actually caught in the act. We don't know where Sergeant appeared from, he was just there, waiting for us to leg it and I was the one who got grabbed. This guy was huge, built like a brick outhouse and just as tall. He asked for my name, even though he knew it, then put me over his knee and gave me a good whacking with his truncheon. It really hurt! He then said, "Get off home and tell your dad you've just had a hiding."

I did go home. Alone 'cos my brothers had put their sprint into sixth gear when they saw Sergeant descending on us. Zero to sixty in about two seconds and they were gone. We had been out all day and we were "black bright" as mother used to say. Our faces were perpetually covered with dust and grime during our estate sorties. On entering the house, Dad says to me, "What have you been crying for?"

"Nothing."

It's obvious that I had been crying because my dust covered cheeks were streaky with dried tears.

"Don't tell me nothing. I can see you've been crying. What for?"

"Honest, nothing".

"Look. Stop messing about and tell me why you've been crying. Has somebody been bullying you?"

I saw this as an opportunity to get my own back on Sergeant, but I'd forgotten that Dad knows absolutely everybody on the estate. I told who had given me a hiding.

"Oh, yea? What for?"

"Nothing."

"If you tell me nothing again, I'll give you a hiding. Sergeant wouldn't have given you a hiding for nothing. You must have been doing something wrong. What was it?"

I told him. He looked at me and paused for a long time... All of about five seconds, then he said to me, in a kindly, caring manner, "Come here a minute." I did and he put me over his knee and gave me my second hiding. Not for stacking bin lids, I'd already been punished for that, but for getting caught!

It was like that in those days. You got caught, you got a hiding and you took your punishment. Nothing more to be said, you moved on...

CHAPTER 3
Bill's School Photo Club

I'm eleven years old and in the final year of Birley Spa Junior School. I'm getting prepared to move up a school to a secondary or grammar school and I'm supposed to be studying for my eleven-plus exam, but I didn't have any inclination for exams at this stage.

My mind was on my hobby and my developing body parts, especially the body part that persistently strained against my underpants. My testosterone levels were rising and I was beginning to take an interest in girls!

For my birthday dad gave me an old camera that he had been given by some bloke for doing the bloke a favour. It meant that I would spend my pocket money on film but I went around pointing and clicking and generally annoying those close to me.

Instead of taking the films to a shop to be developed I joined the school's camera club. That way I knew that I would get my photos developed for free as the school provided everything required to develop film. But I had to learn how to do it.

In today's digital age you don't need any of this developing stuff. You take your pictures and you either store them on your mobile phone until you delete them 'cos you've run out of memory, or you send them to the 'cloud' to be later hacked by some unscrupulous geek. Alternatively, you plug your camera into a printer and print off grainy photos on cheap photocopy paper.

So, what stuff did the camera club need for photo development? Well, in those days it required certain chemicals, special paper and specific equipment. Most importantly of all, film processing required a dark room in which to keep one's chemicals, paper and equipment and, indeed, in which to develop the film. The dark room must be absolutely pitch black. All light had to be prevented from entering this room because photo film was light sensitive and your photos would be ruined, obliterated even, if light got on the film while you are processing it.

At this juncture you should, perhaps, be given some idea of the initial process of film development.

You require a small, circular developing tank inside of which you put a spiral reel. When the light goes out in the darkroom you have to carry out the first procedure, which is to remove your film from its cartridge and wind it onto the spiral reel. This is then placed inside the developing tank, the lid is secured on this and you are now ready to add your chemicals. All this is done by feel because the room is in absolute pitch-black darkness. When the tank lid has been tightly screwed on you can now turn the light back on. Now this procedure takes about five to ten minutes depending on how good you were at loading the spiral reel.

Something else absolutely essential to film processing at school was a big cardboard box of biscuits 'cos you might get peckish during your lesson. The biscuits were packed three to four in little cellophane packets which cost three [old] pence (3d).

Camera club lessons usually took place after school and they were a great wheeze. Three or four boys... And sometimes girls, crowded into the school's darkroom, a converted cupboard decked out with benches to work on and shelves to keep things on. The biscuits were kept on one of the top shelves.

Because the room's interior was somewhat restricted by the benches, anyone not loading their spiral reel had to sit on one of these benches, out of the way of "Miss" and her pupil. When the lights went out one of three things happened.

1. You quietly, and I mean ultra-quietly, lifted the lid of the biscuit box and put two or three packets of biscuits in your satchel for later, or...

2. You explored the girl's developing breast because you knew she wouldn't say anything until playtime next day, when she would brag to her friends about how she had "done it", or...

3. Both.

Doing any one of these things was a bit of a gamble because the light could be turned on at any time, unexpectedly. So, when you started screwing the lid on your tank you had to signal your mates that light turning on time was close. Sometimes a cough would do the trick, assuming this was the signal you had agreed beforehand. At other times you declared, "Just screwing the lid on, miss."

Now my rogue gene was not one to pass up on an opportunity and one evening I got the shock of my life. I almost dropped through a huge fissure that suddenly opened up in the floor! Seriously!

One of my mates had been going to camera club for ages and he was adept at loading the spiral reel. He could be left to it without any supervision. I knew that he would stretch the time required to load his reel, because we had agreed to this earlier. What I didn't know, however, was that on this particular evening, when the light went out "Miss" had silently made the girl sat next to me budge up to give her room to sit on the bench.

I think you can see where this is going, can't you?

In pitch blackness my hand went across to explore what I thought was going to be a semi-flat chest, but instead I got a huge handful.

I silently thought "What the...?" After a second (Or two? Or perhaps even three?) I felt "Miss'" hand on mine gently removing my cupped fingers from her breast. Not one word was said. When the light switch was flicked on, I turned to see precisely who I had just groped. Not expecting "Miss" to be sat next to me I looked horrified, aghast, feeling my face all hot, blushing a crimson colour. Still no word.

When camera club finished for the evening "Miss" held me back while the rest of the pupils filed out of the darkroom. I thought, "This is it. I'm gonna get chucked out of school for this."

Seeing the obvious embarrassment on my face "Miss" just smiled and said, "Billy, if you're going to do that you should make sure you know who you're doing it to."

With that she let me go, and each and every time we met in class during the daytime she just carried on as if nothing had happened. I bet she had a few good laughs in the staff room about it, though.

And I bet my rogue gene was disappointed with that outcome...

*

One of my earliest memories of rogue gene interference was after I smacked this boy in the playground for bullying the girls. He was a proper pest, continually lifting the girl's skirts and trying to "tweak" their non-existent breasts.

Maybe his testosterone levels were more prevalent than the other boys, but that was no excuse for causing such distress. Anyway, I told him to, "Leave 'em alone!" But he didn't, so not only did he disobey an order, he disrespected me for disobeying my order. Something had to be done to calm him down and I took the initiative, much to the girls' gratitude and much to the irritation of my rogue gene.

Ordinarily, the kid would have picked himself up, called me a few choice names and got on with life. I think I may have already told you this, but it was like that then. You got caught, you got a hiding and you took your punishment. Nothing more to be said, you moved on.

Unfortunately for me his nose bled, probably in response to my rogue gene's influence on his rogue gene. It wasn't a serious bleed but he made a meal of it and the duty playground teacher sent us both to the headmaster's office for fighting. Today, the guy would have been bandaged, mollycoddled and stretchered to hospital and I would become attached to a policeman's arm. But in those days, you just got sent to the headmaster.

Now we've all seen old television programmes where a schoolboy gets his arse whacked for doing something wrong. Remember programmes such as 'Whack-O!', a British sitcom TV series starring Jimmy Edwards (Broadcast from 1956 to 1960 and 1971 to 1972), or Billy Bunter of Greyfriars School,

31

a BBC television show (broadcast from 1952 to 1961)? These programmes were true to life! We really did get our arses whacked, and with a whole range of implements. Depending on the severity of our transgression you were whacked with a slipper, a shoe with a hard sole, or a cane.

Anyway, after a reprimand by the Head, the other boy was sent away to clean himself up and join his class. I was preparing myself for a whacking.

The Head told me to go outside his office to the corridor, where there was room for him to swing his arm, while he got his whacking slipper out, and he told me to, "Get downstairs," and wait for him. Now what do you suppose he meant by that? Well, I took his instruction literally and headed for the staircase.

I'd have loved to have seen his face when he emerged from his office carrying his whacking slipper, to find the corridor empty.

The staircase led to a large hall where the Head held assembly. Today there was a girl's class doing PT in knickers and vests. As soon as I walked in everything went quiet and everyone looked in my direction.

"What do you want, Billy," the teacher asks.

"The head's just sent me downstairs, miss."

"Oh? Why?"

"Don't know miss. He just told me to 'get downstairs'."

"And he didn't say why?"

"No miss."

My face took on a puzzled look at the head's unfathomable instruction to get downstairs. Why on earth did he want me to go to the girls' PT class?

"Well, you'd better get back to your own class. I'll see

what the head wants, when I've finished here."

"Yes, miss."

With a shrug of my shoulders, I went back upstairs to the corridor. It was empty and the head's door was closed. So, I carried on to my own class which was on the other side of the school.

After lunch my class teacher told me that the head wanted to see me.

"What for miss?"

"I don't know, but you'd better get along there to find out."

Off I went... Anything to get out of math class. Along the corridors of learning I arrived at the head's office and gently knocked on the door.

"Come in."

"Sir, my teacher said you want to see me".

"Yes, Billy Pollard. Where did you go when you left here?"

"When was that, sir?"

"After I told you to 'get downstairs'."

"Oh. Then?"

"Yes, Billy. Then. Where did you go?"

"I went downstairs, sir."

"You... You what? You went downstairs? To the hall?"

"Yes, sir. That's where the stairs go," as if he didn't already know this.

"Why?"

"Because you told me to."

"No, I didn't."

"Yes, sir. You definitely told me to 'get downstairs'."

"No... I didn't mean 'get downstairs', I meant 'GET

DOWNSTAIRS'!"

My face took on a look of incredulity that said, "What the hell is this guy on about?"

Before I could say anything else he stands up and repeats "GET DOWNSTAIRS," bending me double with one hand pressing on my stomach and the other pushing my head down.

When he let go, I straightened myself upright and said "Ooooh… that downstairs."

Holding his head in his hands he says, in a resigned way, "Go back to your class, Billy, and don't do it again." What did he mean by that? Don't fight, don't go downstairs, don't do what?

I didn't get a whacking for giving the bully a bloody nose and I smiled as I returned to my class. It sometimes pays to act the goat…

CHAPTER 4
Bill's Unfortunate Nosedives

I've been lucky with "accidents" that result in broken bones.

I once broke my ankle, a Pott's fracture, when I was in the army. During a parachuting exercise I landed on a pile of house bricks some idiot, single brain cell squaddie had left on the DZ (dropping zone) because he was too idle to carry his container (full of house bricks) away. We had to pack our own containers and they had to weigh a minimum forty-five pounds. We used items like bedside lockers or suitcases full of clothes because these had to be returned to your quarters, although a bag of sand was the favourite material for a container because this could be spread out over the DZ without causing any harm to future parachutists.

I now consider that particular breakage as part of the job. But there were a couple of incidences in my younger days, both in the same week, that can only be credited to my rogue gene. In fact, in view of the short period between these incidents, mere days, I must blame my rogue gene who, may I add, decided to make me both harmless and, indeed, armless.

My two elder brothers and I heard that a good Flash Gordon film was showing at our local cinema. This cinema was situated at the bottom of Intake on the way to Manor Top. Taking a number forty-one bus, you went up Birley Spa Lane, right, onto Occupation Lane, right again, onto Birley Moor

Road, past Frecheville shops, down the hill past Linley Lane and there it was. The REX cinema. Whenever we went to the cinema we never went on the bus, though, because we never had the bus fare. Instead, we walked up the fields. It took us twenty times longer, all up hill, but it was cheaper and there was no end of trouble that we almost avoided on the way.

However, we had to find 9d for entry to the cinema for one person, usually eldest brother, plus a bit more for an ice cream and a small bottle of lemonade.

9d? Okay, you young captains of industry. Here's a lesson on "old" money.

Let's start off with one old penny = 1d.

Three old pennies equalled a threepenny bit (pronounced 'threpny') = 3d.

Six old pennies or two threpny bits equalled a sixpenny bit (pronounced 'sixpenny') = 6d.

Twelve old pennies or four threpny bits or two sixpenny bits equalled one shilling or a 'bob' = 1/- or 12d.

Twenty-four old pennies, eight threpny bits, four sixpenny bits or two bob coins equalled a two shilling coin (pronounced, would you believe, 'a two bob bit') = 2/-.

Here's where it gets a bit complicated.

Two single bob coins and a 6d piece equalled a half crown or two shillings and six pence (normally pronounced 2and6) = 2/6d.

Five bobs equalled a crown (normally pronounced 'Five Bob') = 5/-.

Take a breath!

120d or forty threpny bits or twenty sixpenny bits or ten bobs or four half crowns or two crowns made ten shillings (pronounced 'a ten bob note') = 10/-.

It follows, therefore, that 240d or eighty threpny bits or forty sixpenny bits or twenty bobs or eight half crowns or four crowns or two x ten bob notes made a quid note or, put simply, £1.

Five quid notes made £5 (pronounced 'fiver') = £5.

Ten quid notes, or two fivers, made a 'tenner' = £10.

Two tenners made a 'twenty' = £20.

I won't go any further because ordinary people rarely had any twenties given to them in their wages packet or change, and they never, ever, had any 'fifties' (£50 notes). Only the banks had fifties. These never saw the light of day, and if you ever saw a £100 note you must have won the pools.

Interesting or what?

Anyway, my elder brothers and I needed the sum total of 9d for cinema entry plus another 3d for an ice cream plus another 6d for a small bottle of lemonade, enough for one person. 1/6d in total. Where were we going to find that?

Up on Birley Spa Lane there was a row of shops, one of which was a newsagent. The three of us went round to the back of this newsagent and one of us crept through the rear gate into the newsagent's yard, where the shop keeper stacked into crates all the empty pop bottles that had been returned to him. If you returned empty pop bottles you got 3d for each empty bottle. The shopkeeper subsequently had some deal with the pop suppliers to return these for cleaning, re-filling and re-labelling.

He who crept into the rear yard passed out six of these empty bottles to his two brothers, waiting behind the rear wall of the yard, then we legged it round to the bus stop on the opposite side of the road to the shop to decide when to return the empties to the shopkeeper via the front door. It would be a bit too obvious if we all went in at the same time, so we picked a time when the shop was really busy and "returned" our empties, two each at varying intervals, to the counter. Six bottles, each with a return value of 3d gave us 18d, or 1/6d, precisely the amount we needed for our cinema trip.

Now you might ask, "Why only enough for one person?" Well, my eldest brother, it was usually him, paid for a stalls ticket at the booth, bought an ice cream and a bottle of pop at the sweet counter then took up a seat as close the emergency exit as possible. This door was behind a thick curtain. When the lights went out for the Pearl and Dean adverts followed by Pathe News in black and white, he crept on all fours behind the curtain and let us in. We then crept up to the balcony and got a seat in the front row. It had to be the front row of the balcony because, during the interval, we could drip lemonade and melting ice cream on unsuspecting heads below. Great fun, lots of laughs and two of us got to see the film for free.

On one cinema trip we got caught "dripping" over the balcony wall. Somebody had complained and, much to the audience's annoyance and protestations, the projectionist stopped the film and turned the lights on. As we were the only ones on the front row of the balcony the drips of ice cream must have been us and the cinema manager chucked us out… Not for the dripping, but for not having a balcony ticket.

So, we set off for home.

In the very bottom of Intake dip, on the right-hand side when going to the city centre, there was an abandoned slag heap. This was where they used to dump all the slag created by the processing of coal from Woodhouse pit.

On the way home from the cinema, that day, my brothers and I climbed this slag heap and played on the top. Having got absolutely filthy from head-to-foot with coal dust it was time to go home and the two elder brothers decided to roly-poly down the slope. When I tried this my roly-poly (Or was it my rogue gene?) got completely uncontrollable and I smashed down the slope into a pile of debris that had been fly-tipped by some inconsiderate lout. When I stood up my right arm, below the elbow, was all floppy and numb. Eldest brother inspected it and decided that perhaps we should let Mum have a look at it. Mum was a nurse during the war.

On arrival at home, Mum says, "Just look at the mess you boys are in. What have you been doing?"

"Nothing, Mum."

"Well, you two can get in the bath…" pointing to elder brothers, "… And Billy can get in the sink." We usually shared the bath water when we had a bath, but in this instance, Mum had decided that the bath water from my elder brothers would deposit more muck onto me than it would take off, so the sink was the next best thing for my bath. Clothes off, I stood in the sink while mum hosed me down with the hose from the washing machine attached to the cold tap. When all the coal dust had disappeared down the plug hole she washed me down with carbolic soap, the only type she bought 'cos it "killed all the germs". Down my shoulders, on to my arms, then, "What the bloody hells happened to your arm?" seeing it flop about uncontrollably.

"What have you been doing?"

"Nothing, Mum."

She makes a close inspection and shouts to Dad, "Bill, I'm going to have to take our Billy to the hospital to get his arm looked at!" No reply, but Mum dressed me in some clean clothes and off we went. On the bus to hospital, I had to give her chapter and verse of our day's outing on the slag heap — nothing about the cinema, though! "Well, that serves you right for getting up to no good on the slag heap," she says. Elder brothers made their own tea that day.

After an X-ray, we found out that I'd got a "Greenstick Fracture" which required a "pot". With a plaster cast weighing down my arm, we went home. Dad looked at the "pot" and grinned. "Serves you bloody right!" he says to me. Everything in those days was "bloody".

Three days later our gang went to pick up a bike for me, given to me by some bloke my dad had done a favour for. The seat was too high but as long as I pedalled standing up it was manageable. I shouldn't have been riding it with my arm in a pot, but it was all downhill to our home so I didn't need to pedal too much and I could use my good arm to steer and brake. It was the first two-wheeler that I'd ever ridden so the trip was a bit shaky, to say the least. My elder brothers both had racers but they throttled back a bit to let me keep up.

We decided to go the long way round; all the way down Occupation Lane instead of turning left onto Birley Spa Lane, onto Sheffield Road and then left onto Main Street to home. The idea was to get me used to my new bike. Half way down Occupation Lane eldest brother stops. He points out a neat pile of straw bales that the local farmer had constructed in preparation of transporting these to the farm. He was in the field, with his tractor pulling a flatbed trailer half loaded with straw bales and on seeing us he waved us into the field. He knew that straw bales were like massive magnets for kids on the estate and didn't mind us playing on them.

"Let's go make a den," eldest brother says, leaning his bike on the fence partitioning the field from the pavement. He hurdles over the fence with one leap without touching it. Next eldest brother takes the same route and in the same way. Okay, if they can make the field in one leap, so can I. Nope! Not even close! My toe caught the top rail of the fence and I literally nosedived into the field. Splat! Head first onto the hard ground, followed by my left shoulder and a somersault onto my back. It all happened in about two seconds. I sat there for a minute and watched my brothers racing towards me.

"Are you OK?" asks eldest brother.

He looked a bit worried because on our way out of the house dad had ordered, "Look after him," pointing in my direction. I confirmed that I was okay, much to eldest brother's relief, and stood up.

"What's wrong with your arm?" I was asked. I looked at my pot and saw that it was dirty, but still in one piece.

"No, not that arm, your other one."

I couldn't see, or feel, anything wrong with my left arm and I turned my head towards my brothers, with a puzzled look on my face. What I didn't realise was that my left shoulder was markedly lower than my right, and both brothers said it wasn't like that when we left home. I told them I didn't know what they were talking about, but eldest brother suggested that perhaps Mum ought to take a look at it, so we finished our bike rides home.

While Dad is adjusting my bike seat, Mum says to us, "Upstairs and in the bath, you two. I'll wash Billy down here."

While I'm sitting on the sink drainer, getting washed, mum says, "What's wrong with your shoulder?" noticing the unequal horizontal plane of this with the other one.

"Nothing, Mum." I couldn't feel anything wrong, so there was nothing wrong.

"You must have done something, look at the shape of you," although that was impossible without a mirror.

Mum washed my face, then lifted my left arm to wash underneath. There was a distinct jolt and a crunch, with a shout of, "OW!" from me. Mum slowly lowered my arm and carefully felt around my shoulder and neck.

Dad had come back into the house having put my bike in the shed and Mum says to him, "Looks like I'm going to have to go back to the hospital with our Billy to get his shoulder looked at!" No reply, but Mum dressed me in some clean clothes and off we went. On the bus to hospital, I had to give her chapter and verse of our day's outing to the farmer's field. Elder brothers had to get their own tea again that day.

At the hospital, the same A&E doctor looks surprised to see me and says, "You again? Have you got a problem with your pot?" Mum tells him about my mishap at the field and about her findings when she washed me. After another X-ray the doctor informs mum that I had "a broken collar bone".

The same A&E nurse manipulated my collar bone and placed my left arm in a tight sling. She gave me a kiss on the cheek and I fell in love.

What a sight I must have made — my right arm in a dirty, dusty pot and my left arm in a shiny new sling. When I returned home with Mum that night, Dad says, "Serves you bloody right!"

The girls at school, though, mothered me… Sometimes even smothered me! The boys just looked on, envious, not only that I was being mothered, or smothered if I happened to be in the library, but also that I didn't have to do any cross country running, or hockey, or P.T. or gym in the main hall.

Sometime after my second trip to hospital, we kids were

having our tea in the dining room and I heard Mum talking to Dad in the lounge. She was saying what a shame it was that, "Our Billy can't do any cross country running, or hockey, or P.T. or gym."

But Dad says, "It's only temporary. He'll be up and running again in no time."

He turns to Mum and jokes, "I bet he's got a bloody rogue gene".

Now that's when I first heard about my rogue gene!

CHAPTER 5
Bill's Rhubarb Misadventure

It is now 1962.

I'm twelve years old, my eldest brother is fifteen, my next eldest brother is fourteen and my younger brother is ten. For my twelfth birthday dad had given to me a small penknife with a decorative pearl inlay handle. He gave one to all us boys on our twelfth birthday because we were "old enough to look after it and use it sensibly". I've still got mine although the tip broke off one of the blades when I tried to open a tin of paint.

Younger brother was now old enough to join our gang providing we stuck to Dad's instruction to "look after him". The four of us went out during the holidays to see what kind of trouble we could stay out of.

Across the valley, half way up the hill to Woodhouse, there was a shit farm... Sorry, Sewage Processing Plant. This was managed by one of my uncles. We'll call him Uncle J. Being on a hillside, this property was ideally situated to receive all the effluent from Woodhouse without having to provide a pumping station. The sewage merely relied on gravity to slide it through the sewage pipes, downhill, straight to the farm. Once the sewage had been processed the slurry was pumped into a holding pit to settle and dry out. This was later sold to the local farmer to fertilise his fields to grow wheat, in which we subsequently used to take our girlfriends for a "walk". You'll read about our "walks" in the fields, later.

At the end of the processing stage the resultant clean water, and I mean really clean, was then allowed to flow into the river in the valley bottom. Having said that it still smelled like a squaddie's jock strap and we never did see any fish in that river.

We decided, one day, to pay Uncle J a visit. But before doing so eldest brother suggested we visit a place he knew to get something to eat. Great idea, notwithstanding that we each had had, not long ago, three sausages, a panful of scrambled egg, a rasher of bacon, two slices of toast and a bowl of cornflakes for breakfast. Mum liked to keep us fed during the holidays because she never knew when we'd be home for another meal.

Off we went down to the fields, past the sh... Sewage Processing Plant and on towards the bottom end of Woodhouse. After much searching, eldest brother found the 'hidden' path he'd been looking for and he took us through the overgrown foliage, swatting away the hanging branches of the bushes we were crashing through. We emerged into a field the size of a football pitch which was full of ripe, ready-to-pick rhubarb.

Laughing, we all dived into the nearest rhubarb plant and plucked a thick stick to chew on. We used our penknives to chop off the leaf and the bit near the root and we took a bite. Oh no! Our rogue genes — all Pollards have one — had somehow given this luscious rhubarb a sour taste. Worse than sucking on a lemon! Feeling a bit despondent we looked at eldest brother for inspiration, or maybe instruction. He thought for a moment and then told us he had a plan.

We were all to walk to Woodhouse without looking up!

We were to keep our eyes focused on the pavement because there was always the odd penny, or halfpenny, or even sixpenny piece laying in the gutter or on the grass verge bordering the pavement. Sometimes there was even a shilling or, better still, half-a-crown laying there. This loose change had fallen out of people's hands as they counted out money for the ice cream van or bread man, or rag-and-bone-man with his horse and cart. On the way to Woodhouse, we called in to a large open space that was home to a travelling funfair when it arrived in the village... Always guaranteed to hold lots of dropped coins. After only forty-five minutes we had enough change to buy a bag of sugar.

Back at the rhubarb field we made ourselves comfortable and tucked into our fruit feast. Did you know that rhubarb is actually a vegetable? Anyway, we enjoyed our banquet, dipping the chewed end of rhubarb into the bag of sugar until it was time to go get another stick. We sat there and chewed on sugared rhubarb, and talked, and chewed on more sugared rhubarb, for hours.

When it was time to go home, we each picked an armful of rhubarb stalks to give to Uncle J and made our way towards the sh... Sewage Processing Plant, to find him. We went to the office. Not there. We went to the canteen. Not there either so he must be down in the sh... effluent plots. Eldest brother told us to return to "this spot" if we couldn't see Uncle J within ten minutes. He split us up and pointed us in three different directions to find him and off we went.

As instructed, we returned to the spot designated the meeting place by eldest brother. At least three of us returned! Eldest brother, next eldest brother and me. Younger brother was absent! A worried look embraced all our faces as we all repeated Dad's instruction to "look after him" in our heads. Eldest brother quickly determined which direction younger brother had been sent and he frantically chased off to find him, shouting his name as he went. We followed as fast as we could, but eldest brother's panic had given him a sixth gear.

After a few minutes we heard younger brother's plea for help. Dashing towards the cries we were brought to a sudden stop by eldest brother's outstretched arms. About ten yards out was younger brother, up to his waste in a drying slurry pit and slowly sinking. He had a blank look on his face as he envisaged his fate.

After a short pause to think, eldest brother suddenly dashed into the foliage and re-appeared with a long branch that he'd torn from a tall bush. He laid this on top of the slurry and instructed younger brother to "grab hold", but it was out of younger brother's reach. Eldest brother then ran full speed towards younger brother, who was now up to his chest. A couple of steps in he started to sink, but his momentum took him at least half way and with a mighty leap he landed just a few feet from younger brother. Turning to us he shouts, "GET YOUR TROUSERS OFF AND TIE THEM TOGETHER!" As we were doing this, he then instructs us to tie one pair of trousers to the end of the branch. Younger brother is now up to his armpits and crying. Eldest brother is up to his waste.

Next eldest brother pulls in the branch and ties a pair of our trousers to it. He then walks forward until he is ankle deep in the mire and he throws the branch towards eldest brother, javelin style. Eldest brother grabs the end and holds out his hand to younger brother who grabs this and starts to pull himself towards eldest brother. With younger brother now hanging round eldest brother's neck, next eldest and I begin to tow the branch back using our trousers, with eldest hanging on to the other end. My two brothers slowly inched their way towards us until eldest could kneel down without sinking too much. He passed younger brother to next eldest who then passed him to me. I carried younger brother to safety while next eldest helped eldest out of the pit.

It was a close call, but we did it. We had saved younger brother!

Our final task was to clean all the slurry off our bodies, and our clothes, before we could even think about going home. Uncle J suddenly appeared from the direction of the canteen. He had a puzzled look on his face and asked, "What the bloody hell have you boys been up to?"

Next eldest brother looked at us all and, with a smile on his face he replies, "We've just been for a swim."

Uncle J marshalled us back to the canteen where there was a hose hanging on the wall. He hosed us down, naked, with clean water, and he then scrubbed our clothes to remove all the slurry. He didn't ask us any questions. Having seen the branch, with our trousers tied to it, he must have guessed what we had been up to.

We dried our clothes in front of the canteen stove as several other workmen made tea and plied us with biscuits. When our clothes were reasonably dry, we set off for home, after firstly gathering up our armfuls of rhubarb. We offered these to the workmen but they graciously declined our offer, so we thought Mum might like the rhubarb to make some rhubarb and ginger jam.

Mum was pleased with the rhubarb. She never asked where we got it and I often wonder what the farmer thought when he went to harvest his rhubarb and found half of it gone, with a pile of rhubarb leaves in its place.

"What the bloody hell have you lot been doing? You smell like nothing on earth."

My brothers and I all piped up in unison, "Nothing, Mum."

"Oh? Well, you can just go and wash that 'nothing' off your bodies with a bath before tea!"

"Yes, Mum."

Nice and clean after our bath, we went downstairs for tea. Dad came in from work and the first thing he asks was, "What's that bloody smell?" In those days everything was "bloody". That smell stayed with us for days, but even more frustratingly was the fact that we couldn't taste anything. Nothing at all. Not even our favourite dinner, mum's famous meat and potato pie. Literally everything we ate for over a week tasted bland, like water. In fact, not even water tasted like water.

We had eaten so much rhubarb that our taste buds had effectively been neutralised!

Something else that we had to thank our rogue gene for...

CHAPTER 6
Bill playing with fire

I think I've told you that I was born in Sheffield, Yorkshire. Do you know that Yorkshire is the centre of the universe? Well, it is, but I might have already told you that, also.

One of the most important rules in life, that kids are taught is, "Don't play with matches!" If you've never taught your kids not to play with matches you should, although by the time this book is finished, I guess that matches may well be obsolete. Who knows?

Anyway, in my younger years I found matches to be a useful commodity. They were ideal for lighting cigarettes, setting fire to kindling in your hearth, burning rubbish in the back garden and, not least, for starting fires in the fields. Now don't go getting the idea that I'm a serial arsonist, 'cos I'm not. But during the long summer holidays my brothers and I had a lot of fun playing with fire. Sit back and relax while I explain.

Hackenthorpe, where I was brought up, is situated on a hill. The hillside gently slopes down to the bottom of a valley where a river lazily meandered its way south towards Staveley and on to Chesterfield. We once followed this river all the way to Chesterfield and got to its end. It just stops. I don't know where it goes next 'cos it just disappeared into the ground.

Spoiler alert! Rogue gene on the prowl.

It took us hours, it was beginning to get dark, and having got as far as Chesterfield we suddenly realised that none of us had any bus fare home. My eldest brother blamed my next eldest brother who made it abundantly clear that I... Me... Should have brought my pocket money to pay for the bus fare. Not that I had any pocket money, anyway, but you know that Yorkshire blokes don't like to admit to a failure! And anyway, only my rogue gene knew we would be meandering, with the river, down to Chesterfield when we left home that morning.

So, we eventually found the A619 out of Chesterfield, which would take us to the A6135 Sheffield Road, and we stuck out a thumb to hitch a lift. We knew this route because we often cycled down to Chesterfield to get something for Mum or Dad... It was the only place that sold it, whatever it was. In those days motorists had absolutely no reluctance in stopping to give hitchers a lift because all hitchers, of all ages and all ethnic leanings could be trusted not to rob you and hijack the car. Especially if the hitchers were kids, like us, and they were from Sheffield. Further, the drivers themselves could be trusted to 'get you home safely'. Sadly, not so, today.

Anyway, back to my homily.

The opposite side of the valley to Hackenthorpe rose quite steeply to a village called Woodhouse and in between Woodhouse and Hackenthorpe there was an abandoned pit head. My great, great, great granddad — the one who came face-to-face with his rogue gene and met his end at Lundhill

Colliery — once worked in this pit, and the abandoned pithead and its surrounding fields were our playground.

Hackenthorpe, the estate, took up a small area of the hillside. The rest of the land, between the estate and the valley bottom, was taken up with large fields separated by narrow footpaths leading to Woodhouse. The local farmer owned these fields and he cultivated them to plant wheat. Towards the end of the summer, around August/September time, the arrival of Pied Piper in the form of a combine harvester gathered all us kids from the estate and led them down to the fields to harvest the wheat. What a spectacle. Hundreds of kids playing in the straw left behind after the harvester had stripped all the ears of wheat from the stalks. Sadly, you don't see that nowadays.

Now the farmer always left a strip of wheat about four or five yards wide unharvested at the bottom of the fields. We never knew why, but this strip of untouched wheat made an ideal place to hide, especially if you took your girlfriend down to the fields for a "walk" or something. This "secret place" was handed down to each generation and the Pollards were not the only ones eagerly awaiting harvest time so they could creep up on the couples "just talking" in the unharvested wheat. The couples always took some loose straw to their hideaways to make their "talk" a little more comfortable. Better to "talk" on a bed of straw than on the hard ground, eh?

It is at this time, when the couples are well into their "discussion", that we quietly stalked to the bottom of the valley and along the footpath running parallel to the field. We then crawled back up to the den that the couples had made for their "chat". Absolute silence on our part was of paramount importance. We didn't want to tip off the couples that we were stalking them, military fashion.

Out comes our matches and striking them on a nearby stone we lit the pile of straw used as bedding by the couples. Giving it a few seconds to build up some smoke we wafted this towards the couple, at the same time jumping to our feet shouting, "FIRE! FIRE! FIRE!"

Suddenly about three or four disturbed and alarmed couples jump up at various locations, the girls in a tizz 'cos their zips had jammed and the boys busily pulling up trousers and pushing on shoes and socks. The inevitable threat "I'M GONNA GET YOU POLLARD AND MAKE YOU SUFFER!" was heard being bellowed at us with fists raised in the air as we ran down the hill, but nothing ever happened to us. Great fun.

The fire quickly spread to the rest of the loose straw further up the field, but Pied Piper MK2, in the form of a small fire engine, always arrived to put the fire out, followed by hordes of kids eager to talk to the firemen. There was always one kid who ran up to a fireman holding the nozzle of the hose jetting water onto the piles of burning straw, who asks, "Wot yer doin' mister?" as if it wasn't obvious. As long as we didn't get in the way the firemen never minded us being so close and asking questions. They even hosed all the soot and smoke debris from us when the fire had been extinguished. Great fun.

When we got home, Mum would always ask "Have you been making fires again?"

"No, Mum."

"Oh? You look like you need a bath."

"Yes, Mum."

Off we tripped upstairs, laughing about our recent, most successful adventure.

*

One day, during the Easter break, a girl from my class at school met me in our street and asked if I wanted to go for a "walk". The answer had to be a nonchalant, "Okay," 'cos this "walk" would surely be more interesting than the usual "walks" up to the library for a fumble that us boys usually endured. And this particular girl was a cracker! She lived in a different street to me and she was keenly desired by most of the boys in our class, although we all knew that we would never stand a chance of "walking" her to the library. She had too much "style" and she came from one of the "rich families" of the estate.

I didn't realise, at the time, precisely what I was letting myself in for... Or what my rogue gene had in store for me.

Arms around each other's waists, we walked down to the field and found a nice quiet spot in a corner somewhere. Hidden by the bushes bordering the field she turns to me and smiles. That smile was hypnotic. She stood about three steps away from me and after a small pause she reaches up behind her back and I hear her zip being slowly pulled downwards. At fifteen years old and brimming with testosterone I stood there speechless. In awe. In a total trance as she let her dress fall to the ground. Until then I had never seen such a thing of beauty, standing there in her bra and pants. She was gorgeous. She was the closest thing to an angel I had ever imagined.

Laughing, she moves towards me and says, "Now it's your turn," and she begins to fumble with my belt.

I silently thought, "YES!" and took the opportunity to carefully slide the straps of her bra down her shoulders to expose more of her "assets" while she's delving around inside my underpants.

We start to kiss… And grope… And we were just getting into the zone when somebody shouted, "OI!"

Surprised, to say the least, we stepped away from each other and this towering, house sized bloke appears through the bushes. He must have been at least twenty feet tall and just as wide, and both the girl and I knew who it was immediately his frame shadowed over us. It was one of the school bullies. A fourth-year student like us and he thought he was God's gift to all the girls at the school. He was also under the false impression that nobody could disagree with anything he said.

Ignoring the angel with very little clothes on standing next to me, he grabs a handful of my hair — from my head, may I add — and tows me to a nearby tree. "Stay there!" he orders and turns towards the girl who, by now, was frantically trying to get dressed. Laughing, he grabs the front of her bra and literally rips it from her shoulders. I thought, "No you don't!" and hurled myself at him just as he was trying to tear her pants from her near naked body. Grabbing him around his neck I pulled him off the girl but this gigantic Goliath merely shrugged me off his shoulders and punched me in the stomach, then on the side of my head. I knew I couldn't stop this guy doing exactly what he wanted but as I was dizzily getting to my feet for another try his rogue gene got the surprise of its life as my eldest brother appeared from nowhere.

Eldest brother had been for a "walk" with his girlfriend when he heard this commotion emanating from the corner of the field, right where those bushes were being disturbed. He'd come over to see what all the shouting was about and he'd seen this animal whack me around the head and make towards a half-naked girl crying for him to, "Stop it! Gerroff me!"

Grabbing the "perp" by his shirt collar and bringing him to an emergency stop, eldest brother quietly says to me and the girl, "Get dressed and go home." We bundle our clothes up and silently walk away from the scene. We didn't look back. We didn't speak as we got dressed half way up the hill, and we didn't look at each other. We went our separate ways home.

Mum said to me, "You've been crying, haven't you?"

"No, Mum."

"Oh? You look like you need a bath."

"Yes, Mum."

I turn toward the stairs and, head hanging low, made my way to the bathroom.

School re-started for the new term.

The girl never returned to our school and I never saw her again. I think her family moved away from Hackenthorpe shortly before the start of the new term. I never found out if she was okay. I never got to take her for another "walk" and I never got to hold her in my arms again. I still daydream about her and about what could have been.

The twenty-foot-tall God's gift to girls never returned to school, either. I heard, some months later, that he had had to go into hospital towards the end of the school holiday for some important operations. Someone said. "For corrective surgery, or something," but we never found out what needed "correcting". Neither did I ever see him again…

CHAPTER 7
Bill's Dilemma

August, 1965.

I knew that I wasn't going back to school because I'd told them that before I left in July. What was I going to do for a living? Dad was beginning to ask, "Have you thought about a job yet?" No pressure, eh? But I had been struggling with a dilemma.

To answer this question, we must turn back the clock to 1961.

I was eleven years old. I'd failed my eleven-plus exam the previous year and I had just started school at Carter Lodge Secondary Modern School. I don't know why they put the 'Modern' bit in its title 'cos the school had certainly been there since we moved to Hackenthorpe about twenty thousand years ago. Eldest brother went there, next eldest brother went there and now it was my turn.

When I got there, it became obvious that the Pollards were well known at this school. For what, I didn't find out until I'd been given the chance to settle in. Sister and younger brother both went to Thornbridge Grammar School, up near Frecheville, 'cos they had passed their eleven-plus, but my rogue gene had other thoughts about my future.

During the first term we tolerated a "concert" at assembly, played on a Cornet, a Tenor Horn and a Euphonium. The piece that was played was easily forgettable.

Until then I hadn't shown any inclination towards music in any way whatsoever but listening to that Cornet and watching the performance something stimulated a couple of brain cells and I thought, "I want to do that."

I went to the music teacher after assembly and asked if he had another Cornet that I could borrow. "Can you play?" he asks, with gleeful anticipation.

"Not yet," I replied. He went to a cupboard and took out a battered Cornet case and handed it to me with the words "Look after it." I took it home, much to Mum's surprise and Dad's trepidation, and admired the instrument in my bedroom. Out of interest I stripped it down and reconstructed it to see how it worked.

I then taught myself to play it. It took me a mere two weeks to learn the fingering and play a few scales. The sound left much to be desired, to the family's distress, but it was a start. With time and practice I became a skilled and proficient Cornet player. Then the Euphonium player left school to become a bricklayer. The music teacher asked me if I would play the Euphonium in the school band. Why not? The fingering was the same, the clef was the same and the music was the same, so I gave it a go and I got good at it. I joined a brass band; The Meersbrook Prize Brass Band. They rehearsed over a pub in the city centre, convenient for the older members of the band, and I became an even better Euph player. I played in many contests around the country with Meersbrook. They were good. I was good.

Such was my want to play music I even joined the Salvation Army band at Woodhouse to get more practice, although I declined to take part in their prayer sessions because

Mum had told me that I was a Methodist.

In my third year at Carter Lodge Secondary Modern School the school band was invited to attend a three-day training course at a Buxton college, all costs paid by the local council. Off we went on the bus to Buxton, all six of us. By now the school band had expanded to two Cornets, a Flugel Horn, a Tenor Horn, a Euphonium (Me), and a Tuba. When we arrived, we found that we were part of a massed band of eighty plus players from all corners of the county. Great sound, great fun, and oh so many girls.

During that year Meersbrook music director took me to one side and told me that as good as I was on the Euph, I would be a better Trombone player, with a richer tone. "Would I consider changing?" The next day, at school, I asked the music teacher if the school had a Trombone. They had, and I took it home with a Tune-A-Day tutoring book and taught myself to play the Trombone. I got good at playing the Trombone.

The following year, my fourth at Carter Lodge, we were again invited to the Buxton three-day course. Now this course consisted of pure music playing. No maths, no P.E., no English, no French. Just playing all day, and with a bit of luck some "playing" at night! The first day was taken up with assessments to determine where we would sit in the band. I was chosen to play top Trombone. Assessment was followed by group practice with the pieces we were to play at a concert on the final day. The second day we had individual practice until break time (ten a.m.) then more group practice. After lunch we had full band practice. On the third day we had full band all day and then we were sent away for tea while the organisers prepared the hall for our concert.

We were instructed to muster at six thirty p.m., dressed in

our best school uniform and with clean and polished instruments. When I entered the hall, I was mesmerised by the lights and microphones hanging from the gantry above the stage. The auditorium was almost full and buzzing with small talk from the audience and the butterflies in my stomach began to dance. We took our places on the stage and the Director of music introduced each school by getting the schools' respective players to stand up. He then dropped a bombshell on the band by announcing, "Tonight the BBC will transmit the concert live on national radio." There was an excited hum from both the band and the audience, and I silently told myself not to fluff my solo. The concert was a success.

The following morning, while we were waiting for the coach to take us to the railway station, I was approached by the course director of music, who I recognised, and another bloke who I didn't recognise. The other bloke was introduced to me as the BBC's Project Manager. He'd been the one who had monitored the airwaves to the BBC during our concert. I was concerned about missing the coach but he said he would get me home. I trusted this guy — you could in those days — and said my goodbyes to my fellow players. The guy told me to wait in the car park.

After about five minutes he re-appeared with his suitcase and placed this in the back of his Jaguar sports car, a two-seater flier. Sheer luxury and a vast improvement on a bus seat.

On the way home he explained that he was impressed with my playing and that he was convinced that I would, one day, find a place in a famous orchestra. But not without hard work and dedication. He said he would like to discuss this with my parents. My butterflies didn't just dance, they pounded the walls of my stomach as if they were trying to escape.

We arrived home at tea time. Dad was there in his overalls, noshing Mum's famous meat and potato pie. He put his plate to one side and invited the guy into the front room. After a nervous pause the guy asked Mum and Dad if they had listened to the radio concert. The answer was no, because they hadn't heard anything about it... We didn't have mobile phones in those days. "That was a great shame," he said and proceeded to let Mum and Dad know what a great concert it was and what a good solo I had played. Mum looked at me with pride. Dad just looked at me.

The guy went on to say that he had contacts in the Royal College of Music (RCM) and that he was sure that he could persuade them to take me in September's intake. Mum and Dad and I were dumbstruck. Silence descended on us all for about a minute, then Dad spoke up with, "And what will it cost us?" The guy said that we would need to contact the college about that, but considered that it would probably be about the same as going to a university. There would be accommodation to pay for and I would need to take my own instrument. Suddenly, my stomach fell through the bottom of my arse and landed with a bump on the floor. We didn't have that kind of money.

Dad asked if there was any alternative to the RCM. After some thought the guy put forward that if I wanted to progress with music professionally, I was too young and inexperienced to apply for orchestral work, as good as I was, but that there was a lot of potential for improvement, in many respects, with the armed forces. Dad's eyes briefly lit up. He had spent nine years in the Royal Artillery during the war years. He'd got two medals and a load of shrapnel in his right leg for his troubles, but he sometimes wished he was back in the army. The shrapnel was his rogue gene's idea of a joke, but it left Dad with a limp and in constant pain.

Our guest gave Dad a business card and agreed that we obviously needed some time to discuss this, and that Dad could contact him any time if we wanted to take up his offer of assistance. After a cup of tea and some broken biscuits he left and I went to my room to think about the enormity of what had been discussed.

As we relaxed that evening, Dad suddenly turned the TV off and told my brothers and sister to go to bed. "Not you, Bill. Me and your mum want a talk with you."

I thought, "Oh great! I'm going to get a bollocking for something." Not so. They'd had a talk and wanted to see what I thought about the guy's proposal. "I don't know," I told them, and Mum reminded me that it would be like going back to school.

Only, "You would be learning music and not maths, or P.E., or English or French."

The music bit piqued my interest, but I volunteered the inevitable question, "How will you pay for it?"

I knew that my parents didn't have two farthings to rub together. I mean this in a literal sense because we still used farthings in those days. It was a quarter of an old penny for you young executives. Anyway, I knew that Mum and Dad just could not afford it at this point in time.

Mum used to make all our clothes. It's true. Shirts, ties, trousers, coats, school uniforms, even two-piece suits. She knitted our socks and pullovers. Underpants and shoes were the only things she bought because she wanted us to be comfortable, although the material she used for our shirts was positively scratchy. She must have used old sacks, or something. Making our clothes wasn't unusual because many mums did the same. Mum also took a cleaning job to supplement Dad's wage and she cooked, washed and cleaned for a bloke and his sons who lived around the corner from us.

Dad. He would come home after a full day's work, dusty, tired and hungry. He was a labourer for Sheffield Council. But instead of relaxing after tea he would go straight out again to "do a favour for a bloke down the road" in exchange for something. Maybe a used saw or hammer, or a couple of shillings, or a bottle of stout "for the missus". I once got a pair of second-hand running spikes via some bloke that Dad had done a favour for. They only lasted a season, but they were better than running in bare feet, and I broke the school records for the one hundred, two hundred and twenty and four hundred- and forty-yard sprints. When Dad's own shoes got a hole in them, he put cardboard inside to save money on repairs.

Despite our abject poverty my parents always, and I mean always, made sure that us kids had decent clothes and shoes to go to school in and that we also had full bellies. Many a time have they gone without meals to ensure that we had something to eat.

Anyway, Mum and Dad tried to persuade me that they would "find the money somehow" if I wanted to go to the RCM. Mum would just have to "find a second job", cooking, washing and cleaning for someone "after teatime", and Dad would work double shifts at weekends and in the evenings.

I knew they were sincere about it, and I also knew that they would support me one hundred percent with any decision I would make. And I knew that somehow, I don't know how, but somehow, they would find enough money to send me to college for four years. But I also knew they would struggle.

And what about my brothers and sister? How long would they have to go without, just so I could go to college?

So that was my dilemma. Do I go to college, at great cost to Mum, Dad and my brothers and sister, or do I join the forces?

After a couple of months at home, several nights of lost sleep and a great deal of thought, and with some regret for what might have been, I made my decision. I would to join the forces.

Dad, at least, was pleased.

Chapter 8
Bill's Struggle to Enlist

September 1965.

I spent that summer mooching around the house, much to Mum and Dad's annoyance. Mum kept on at me to, "Get out from under my feet," or, "Why don't you find something to do?"

Dad just kept on at me to, "Get a job." Elder brothers were now at work so I couldn't even go out to see what kind of trouble to stay out of.

I had struggled with the dilemma of whether to go to college or join the forces, and having decided to join the forces I brooded for a while with thoughts of what unit to join and what life in the forces would be like. One option was the Royal Artillery, Dad's outfit in the war. He would be really chuffed if I chose that bunch but I didn't fancy it. Too noisy and not enough excitement. But it was now time to make a move, if only to stop Mum and Dad going on at me.

I boarded a number forty-one bus and went to the city centre. There were a couple of recruiting offices down town and this was where to start. I wanted a life of music, so whichever branch of the forces I chose, it had to have a band. I had always had a romantic thought of joining the Navy. Seeing different countries, wearing a uniform that was guaranteed to pull the girls, living on a ship on the high seas and making lots of mates. I went to the recruiting office for the Navy. Having stated my specification to the matelot behind the counter he agreed what a wonderful time I would have. He took my name and address and enthusiastically confirmed that, "Someone would be in touch." I returned home to await a contact from "someone".

About a week later I got a letter. My very first letter ever, sent with my name on the envelope. Everyone at home was interested in its contents, although I suspected that ninety percent of their interest was more towards the nosey end of the spectrum. I took it upstairs to read it. Inside was a letter inviting me to Portsmouth for an "assessment" that would include a written test, a medical examination and a guided tour of a ship. A rail ticket was stapled to the letter. I had skipped past the letterhead and gone straight to the meat of the text. Wrong!

Mum and Dad were well chuffed at me joining the Navy but not nearly as much, I suspect, as the free rail ticket I had been sent. On the day mentioned in the letter I boarded the train to Portsmouth to see what this Navy thing was all about. My rogue gene already knew, but never gave me any warning that it was up to no good.

I, and about six others, were met at Portsmouth station and we were taken to the camp in a white bus. On arrival we were then taken to the canteen for a meal, after which we had to line up at the medical officer's (MO) door. Once inside there I was subjected to lot of prodding, poking, touching my toes, touching my nose and, most embarrassingly, having my balls rolled around in the MO's hand and made to cough. I recollect thinking that whilst this guy got paid to roll my balls around there was a multitude of girls at school who would do it for free!

Next stop, gymnasium. We had been given a pair of blue PT shorts and some PT shoes that we could keep and we queued, bare backed, to get in the big double doors. A PT instructor (PTI) ushered us into the gym and for about two hours put us through our paces lifting, touching toes, heaving on beams, running round the perimeter of the room and doing press-ups while he took notes. We were then released to get a shower, have some tea and relax on our beds 'till lights out.

Next day, final day... Morning only 'cos our train back to London was due to leave at four p.m. Following a noisy awakening at six thirty a.m. we were taken for a forty-five-minute run. After a shower we again queued outside the offices and then taken into a large briefing room where we were given a written test. We had a spot of lunch and returned to the briefing room to be told, with great enthusiasm, that we had all been accepted for the Merchant Navy!

"What?" This wasn't exactly what I was thinking. I was more into big guns and hammocks and flashy uniforms that would attract the girls, not tankers or cargo vessels or ferries, and I decided to ask a few questions, like, "What band will I be in?" Sniggers from a couple of the other boys and I thought about the prospects of flattening their noses. I decided against it, not because I wanted to but because the briefing Officer invited me into a room somewhere at the rear while his 2IC continued briefing the others.

We had an interesting chat. Ultimately, we agreed that I should try joining the Royal Navy because they had bands and the Merchant Navy didn't. I was put in a Land Rover and taken to the railway station to catch an earlier train. Mum and Dad were a little surprised at my early arrival back home but they were, nonetheless, sympathetic about my botched attempt to join the forces. Not to worry, I'll try again.

Back to the same recruitment office a couple of days later. I looked at the brochures and decided on the Royal Marines. But first, I should cut out some red tape and enquire about the band before going anywhere else. "Oh yes," the sergeant said. "Lots of bands. Each ship has its own band. They even have a school of music at Deal, in Kent." Just what I wanted to hear, so I agreed to a medical in two weeks' time.

I had the medical upstairs in the same recruitment office. I endured the same prodding, poking, touching my toes, touching my nose and having my balls rolled around in the MO's hand and being made to cough. Then the MO dropped a bombshell. He asked if I had ever been camping. The answer was a most definite, "Yes!" and he asked me all about it. Did I ever sleep in damp clothes while I was camping? "Occasionally," I answered, with some unease.

Quite how I don't know, but this MO had detected that I had, "A little rheumatism in my right knee." It wasn't enough to worry about at this stage but he suggested I see my family doctor. Most disappointingly, though, was the comment that he was unable to approve me for the Marines because of this affliction. With a sigh I left the office and returned home to tell Mum and Dad about this attempt to join up. I didn't go into how much I had cursed my rogue gene on the way home.

I wasn't going to give up, however. Fortunately, the recruitment office for the Army and Airforce was situated on the opposite side of the city to the one I had just tried. Let's see what the RAF has to offer.

In the door, shown to a seat in front of a desk and introduced to an RAF officer. Before anything else, a question from me… "Does the RAF have any bands?"

"Yes, each station has a band that provides music for parades, ceremonies and concerts."

Great. "How do I join?"

I got the usual homily about a written test, a medical and an interview elsewhere and I returned home to await my letter. It arrived about two weeks later, again with a rail ticket, this time to RAF Leeming, North Yorkshire. Being in Yorkshire, which is, we all know, the centre of the universe, I was optimistic that I might be onto a winner here and once again packed my overnight bag for a three-day trip.

I went through almost exactly the same examination process as I endured with my abortive effort to join the Navy and again, during a briefing, I enquired what facilities would be provided for my advancement in music. A short, whispered discussion took place between the two officers providing the briefing and once more I was taken to a small room at the rear of the briefing hall.

It was explained to me that I had just passed the aptitude tests for joining the RAF as a Leading Airman, ground-based crew. I repeated what I had been told about bands in the RAF, by the recruiting sergeant. "He is correct," the officer confirmed. "Most stations do have a band, but these are voluntary bands, a mix of RAF personnel who enjoy playing an instrument, and civvies who also enjoy playing an instrument." There was no specific school of music to teach advancement in music, the bands were part-time bands that, "Practiced one evening each week and sometimes took part in parades, ceremonies and concerts."

I could not believe my luck! Why is my bloody rogue gene making it so difficult for me to join the forces? Another early train ride home.

Mum and Dad were, again, sympathetic — less so than the last time — but I assured them I was not going to give up. The only option available to me now was the Army. This time Dad asserted that he would accompany me to the recruiting office.

Now I may have mentioned, at some stage, that Dad knew absolutely everyone. I mean it. We both went to the Army recruitment office the following day and would you believe it, Dad knew the army bloke sat behind the desk! Don't ask me how, or where, or when, but they greeted each other as though they were lifelong pals. Maybe Dad had done a favour for this bloke. I don't know but I was, nonetheless, flabbergasted.

Dad explained what I wanted out of forces life — most importantly a band, advancement in music, travel, excitement and maybe even the possibility of meeting girls. Without doubt, the guy confirmed that the Army would provide all of that, plus more. He even promised. He then asked what unit was I thinking of joining. I hadn't really thought about that but I had been looking at a poster for the Parachute Regiment behind the recruiting sergeant. "Be positive!" I thought, and without any hesitation I proffered that as my first choice.

He gave me a form to fill in then went off "to make a phone call". Returning, he confirmed that the Parachute Regiment did, indeed, have a band. In fact, they had three bands and there was a vacancy for a trombone player! We had a lengthy discussion, during which he explained about boys' service, The Royal Military School Of Music, parachuting, travel and lots of other things that piqued my interest, and we arranged for a medical and written test in the same office in two weeks' time.

I passed both... I didn't mention the camping bit to the inspecting MO and he seemed to have missed my rheumatism. Maybe he ignored it. Who knows? There and then I was sworn in, given my King's Shilling (I spent that on my bus fare home), the short version Bible I had used to be sworn in (I've still got that) and a free rail ticket to Aldershot.

At last, I could join the forces and my rogue gene didn't interfere. Maybe it was having a day off. Who knows? Maybe it had deliberately engineered my path to joining the Army. Who knows? Who cares? I'm now in the Army.

CHAPTER 9
Bill's Apprenticeship

In October, 1965, I had been sworn in to the Parachute Regiment and given instructions to travel to Aldershot on the 6th January, 1966.

To pass the time between October and January dad got me a job with Sheffield Council as an apprentice joiner. I thought he just wanted me out from under Mum's feet but his reasoning was that a job would instil some worldly knowledge in me before I left home. Further, and perhaps more pertinent, I would be contributing towards my upkeep while at home.

He arranged for me to start work on a project to soundproof a clinic for the deaf in the city centre. This struck me as a bit contradictory. An opposite in terms. Why would anyone want to soundproof a clinic for the deaf when the deaf couldn't hear anything anyway?

Still, I arrived on site nice and early on a Monday morning with the tool bag that Dad had "loaned" me. At the time, my mind wasn't fully on this job, because my thoughts were on joining the army.

This soundproofing project involved attaching two-inch by one-inch battens to the walls and ceiling joists of several rooms. Cross battens were fixed between the mainstays and the square voids created by this procedure were then filled with heavy duty fibreglass insulation. Pegboard was then nailed to the battens with panel pins. Not exactly a technically complicated job, but a job that was, nonetheless, made complicated by a lack of technical equipment. Don't forget, this was 1965 and things like Rawlplugs, electric drills, and cordless screwdrivers were either a figment of someone's imagination or too expensive for the council's budget.

To drill holes in the brick walls we had to use an awl, a tool with a star shaped point and a heavy steel handle. Put the point on the wall where you need a hole, give the awl a hefty whack with a five-pound lump hammer, turn it, then give it another whack and a turn. Repeat this until the hole in the brickwork was deep enough to accommodate a long screw. Sounds easy, doesn't it? Well, it was far from easy. If the awl was just a fraction out-of-alignment the hole just got wider, not deeper, and the handle that you whack was less than half an inch in diameter so you whacked your thumb more often than the awl. There was a definite art in using an awl to drill holes. There was also an art in making the plugs to fill the holes. We had to make these ourselves from bits of spare, or dead, wood using our well-honed chisels. That's where the phrase 'deadwood' comes from. Too big and the plug wouldn't go in the hole. Too small and it waggled around uselessly. It had to be just the right size to tap it into the hole, nice and snug.

I didn't think my rogue gene had enough room to manoeuvre with a procedure as simple as this but rogue gene had other ideas! The holes were too wide or not deep enough.

The battens were not vertical enough. The cross battens were not horizontal enough. The plugs were too loose. Anyway, having eventually mastered the art of fixing battens to the wall, and taking twice as long as it should, I was "promoted" to fixing battens to the ceiling.

This required an entirely different skillset. To fix the mainstays you had to find the timber joists supporting the floor above. You did this by gently tapping the ceiling to find the "sweet spot" where the joist is directly above. That's where you nail the batten. Although there was a bit of skill involved in nailing with the hammer upside down. Quite a lot of the ceiling plaster got pummelled until I mastered that art but that bit was the easy bit. Battens fixed, cross battens fixed and I worked my way across the ceiling. Not too many problems, until I reached the final corner!

Rogue gene kicked into gear and made the task of finishing this job... What shall we say? Problematic.

Nail driven into the batten, ready to "fix" to the ceiling joist. Check. Batten positioned below the ceiling joist and held up, onto the ceiling plaster. Check. Give the nail a clout to drive it into the joist, and what happens? I had misjudged the position of the joist by about an eighth of an inch. The batten was driven up through the ceiling and into the void, and the hammer... Dad's hammer... Got jammed between the batten and ceiling joist. To get the batten, and hammer, back down I had to firstly free the hammer so I gave this a mighty pull. It certainly freed the hammer but in doing so it pulled down about four square yards of battens and ceiling plaster. Covered in plaster dust and tangled up in the battens I lowered myself onto the scaffold platform. With no support from below about another two square yards of cantilevered battens and ceiling plaster dropped down.

The noise brought my boss and a couple of workmen rushing to the room. After a few laughs, at my expense may I add, we all set about repairing the damage created by my rogue gene.

The whole job was finished and rooms were cleaned and sound tested in just over a week. On the same day the project was signed off, Dad collared me at the tea table. He mentioned that I'd earned a reputation for being a good worker and that the following day I was being "promoted" to the maintenance team at a complex known as the Park Hill Flats, a sprawling, multi-storey block of council flats built on the outskirts of the city centre. I honestly don't know how Dad got this information or who he had been talking to but I was aware that Dad knew absolutely everybody in Sheffield and everybody knew him.

The Park Hill complex was built between 1957 and 1961, and in 1998 was given Grade II* listed building status. Dad had been one of the labourers that built this estate. Google it.

My thoughts were still on joining the army but, nonetheless, I was initially given the job of repairing door frames to the flats that had been smashed open by the police, or some angry husband, or a burglar or even a housewife that had forgotten her door key.

My "patch" was the whole of the Park Hill Flats and first thing each morning I reported to the estate manager's workshop, a conversion of two ground floor flats in the centre of the complex. Dropping off my haversack, with my lunchtime sandwiches (generally known as "snap") and my billycan for making tea in, I picked up my daily list of doorframes to repair. The addresses on this list were provided by the tenants who had called to the "office" to report the damage.

This list was "managed" by the estate manager. I say "managed" loosely because this guy did nothing. He sat in the workshop all day, chain smoking himself to death and reading the newspaper and drinking tea. The list was, in fact, "managed" by the tenants who merely wrote their name and address on a pre-printed form attached to a clip board hanging just inside the door. The tenants knew where it was, I knew where it was, and that's all anyone needed to know about this form. I didn't particularly like the estate manager because he exhibited few interpersonal skills, he smelled like a dead dog, he was a bully and he did nothing for the tenants.

The tenants didn't like him either because he exhibited few interpersonal skills, smelled like a dead dog, was a bully and did nothing for them. I became known throughout the estate as a "helpful lad" and the tenants started to ask for me, and not the estate manager. This pissed him off enormously, and he took great strides to ensure that I was aware of that fact. I let Dad know but all he had to say about it was, "Just make sure you're not late for work, and keep your nose clean."

Anyway, off I went each day with my bag of tools that Dad had provided. Dad didn't just have a tool for any job, he had a tool for every job, plus a backup tool in case the one he was using broke, or got blunt. He gave me a selection of his spares with the unforgettable words, "Look after them!"

One morning I arrived at the workshop to find my tool bag had been opened. A cursory glance inside confirmed that a couple of screwdrivers and a claw hammer were missing. Rogue gene's doing? I asked my favourite boss, "Who's been inside my tool bag?"

"I don't know."

"Have you been in my tool bag?"

"No. Why?"

"I've got some tools missing."

"Are you accusing me of nicking them? I'll clip you around the ear if you go around calling me a thief!"

"I'll only call you a thief if you nicked my tools. Did you?"

With that he lashed out with his foot, and missed. Instead of kicking me on the leg he kicked a lawn mower that gave a screech as it was projected about twelve inches across the floor and into the desk, which had his mug of tea on it, which overturned onto his newspaper, and dripped tea all down his open haversack, drenching his snap.

The guy was furious. I quickly picked up my tool bag and made for the door, followed by a spanner that punched the centre of my back. Dropping my tool bag, I turned to face this guy who, by now, had turned a crimson colour and was bellowing at me to, "GET OUT! AND DON'T COME BACK!" I thought about flattening his nose, but decided against it 'cos he was the boss. Picking up my tool bag and haversack I decided to go home.

Now what I didn't know was that Dad always marked his tools with a secret indicator somewhere on the tool to show it was his.

When he returned home from work, he commented about me being early. I explained why. He just said, "Don't worry about it. I'll see to it. Just make sure you turn up for work tomorrow."

The following morning dad left home ultra-early. Mum didn't know why and I didn't press the matter. On arrival at work, I was met by a mate of Dad's and a tenant who was eagerly waiting for his door frame to be repaired. There was no sign of the estate manager. Dad's mate said to me, "Hello Billy. You've just missed your dad."

"Oh? What was he doing here?"

"Don't know. I think he came to see a man about a dog."

Okay. Some explanation is required about "seeing a man about a dog". Basically, it's Sheffield speak and it's another way of saying, "I don't want you to know where I'm going or even where I've been because it's none of your business so I'm not going to tell you."

On collecting my tool bag, I noticed that the missing screw drivers and claw hammer had mysteriously reappeared and were sitting there smiling a welcome at me. Looking round I couldn't see, or smell if it comes to that, the estate manager. I asked Dad's mate where he was.

"Don't know. I think he went to see a man about a dog." I never saw that manager again…

On my return to the workshop for lunch I was met by another manager. This one had clean, smartly pressed overalls on and he greeted me with a smile and a firm handshake. I knew I was going to like this guy and I knew that the tenants were going to like him.

*

Meeting the tenants was a real education, in many more ways than one!

Most of the time I was greeted with, "Who is it?" when I knocked on the door.

Speaking through the letterbox I would confirm,

"Maintenance. I've come to repair your door frame." After a few days on the job word got round that there was "a new lad on the maintenance team and he's very polite and helpful". The tenants even remembered my name. Repairing door frames soon extended to repairing cupboard door hinges and I was always welcomed inside for a cup of tea and a cake.

Other members of the maintenance team had warned me about some of the tenants. Some of them (the tenants) deliberately "forgot" their key, or "fell" onto a cupboard door just to have someone round to talk to while repairs were being carried out. Living in this place, at that time, could be really lonely and the tenants liked nothing better than to drink tea, have a cake and have a good natter. No problem providing you fixed the thing you came to fix.

Sometimes the requisition for repair was a complete fiction. Frequently, while talking through the letterbox, I noticed the silk dressing gown, or baby doll nighty, or partially dressed body and I knew that I would be on thin ice when I entered the apartment. Having been told that the "damage" had already been repaired I would find my way out barred and the dressing gown tantalizingly open. Now at my age, fifteen and a bit, I was almost permanently bursting with testosterone but I knew that if things "got out of hand" I would be out of a job. Possibly... Probably with some husband, partner, boyfriend or father hunting me down for a good kicking. So my philosophy was to "keep my nose clean" by finding a way out, as much as I hated to. I knew that I wouldn't stand a chance against some bruiser that drank molten steel and chewed on concrete during snap time.

There's a knack to getting oneself out of this type of situation. You have to get the woman to think it's her idea that you should leave... Without upsetting her. So, nonchalantly groping her to give her the idea that she is in charge you enjoy the moment... For a long, long moment... Then you suddenly let go and say, "Who's that at the door?" The woman immediately steps back, miraculously discovers her dressing gown cord and tidies herself up. I make my way to the door with a mental note that this apartment houses deep, deep trouble.

During my time working at these apartments, I've been ambushed by frustrated housewives, schoolgirls who want to improve their ratings at school, lonely grannies who just want to pass the time, prostitutes, druggies who just want some cash for their next fix, men dressed in all sorts of weird garments and even women with their daughters to make a threesome. A good grounding for a life in the army, eh? Perhaps that was Dad's plan all along?

Reluctantly handing in my week's notice I decided that I should at least say my goodbyes to some of the more 'welcoming' tenants. After all, they had given me an open invitation to go back for some more tea and cake...

The maintenance team gave me a good send-off. They nailed my overalls to a door for the day while I was still wearing them. They fed me at lunchtime, they tied a balloon onto my penis so that I could have a piss and they took some photo's... All in good spirits.

With a touch of sadness, I left work on the 5th of January to go join the army the following day.

BOOK 2
BILL'S ARMY LIFE

CHAPTER 10
Bill's 1, 23 1

6th January, 1966, arrived and Mum packed just one change of clothes into an old holdall that Dad had been given for doing some bloke a favour. Dad insisted that I needed only one set of spare clothes because I would be issued with a uniform when I got to Aldershot. He was partially correct. Despite Dad's insistence that we would not need any civvy clothes, we were allowed out at the weekends so we did need some decent clothes to chat up the Aldershot girls.

Anyway, on the 6th January, Mum and Dad went with me to Victoria Station, Sheffield city centre, to catch the train suggested by the recruitment sergeant. With more than a sense of excitement I chatted non-stop all the way to Sheffield on a number forty-one bus. Mum responded with a frequent, "Yes, love," while Sad just sat behind us watching the pavement rush by.

We were about thirty minutes early for the train. That was Dad's doing 'cos he always arrived, and I mean always, thirty minutes before any appointment he had, to make sure he was on time. He was never late for anything and he had a reputation for being on time. I, also, learned to "be on time" while I was in the army.

Anyway, we all waited for my train on platform one and during our wait, Dad gave me a lecture on keeping my nose clean — that is to say keeping out of trouble — keeping my clothes clean, keeping my body clean and keeping myself to myself. "Don't stand out in a crowd or you'll make a fool of yourself," were his words of wisdom. With those words I boarded the train, pulled the window down and watched Mum and Dad grow smaller as we pulled out of the station. Mum waved to me until the train made her disappear round a corner and I couldn't help feeling a sense of nostalgia. Actually, it was more a sense of loss in the knowledge that I was now no longer a permanent member of my family. No more stacking bin lids. No more playing with fire. And no more "walks" up to the library or down to the fields.

But I'm now part of a bigger family.

I arrived at St. Pancras and after negotiating the underground I arrived at Waterloo Station to await my train to Aldershot. To pass the time while waiting for the Aldershot train, about thirty minutes, I flirted with some girls who were waiting for the same train. We boarded the Aldershot train and we found out that we were all going to join the Army, in the girls' case The Women's Royal Army Corp (WRAC) at Guildford. We couldn't swap addresses because we didn't know where to write to, yet. This was a great shame because I think one of the girls fancied me and she was a real cracker. Gorgeous. She kept blowing kisses to me. Maybe she was just teasing but I couldn't help thinking, "What a waste, joining the army looking like that." If only we had had mobile phones in those days.

On arrival at Aldershot station I, and another eight or nine boys, were met by a white single decker bus similar to the one that met me when I went for the navy tests. I wondered if this was the same bus? We were taken to our new home, The Junior Parachute Company (JPC) at Malta Barracks (Bks). We called it The Jungle Patrol Company because it fooled all the girls... Well nearly all, into thinking we were hardened paratroopers. Most of the time we shot ourselves in the foot by telling the girls we lived in Malta Bks, and they knew just who lived in Malta Bks!

These barracks were a collection of wooden billets (huts) housing eleven boys each. The "camp" was located in the middle of a small forest, with the Basingstoke canal running alongside the camp's boundary. All new entrants had to be housed together until they had passed their admission cadre (squad), yet more written tests and medicals. I was beginning to get used to some stranger caressing my balls, but I still didn't like it! Anyway, I couldn't do anything about it 'cos this bloke was a 'Sir', and we had to do what 'Sir' told us 'cos he was a 'Sir'.

Now, the first thing I learned when I settled in to my new home was how to count up to three. For some reason this number featured heavily in the Army's vocabulary. My regiment for example, The Parachute Regiment, had three battalions; 1 Para, 2 Para and 3 Para. To help us remember how many battalions we had, they all had names; Sporting 1, Shiny 2, Gungy 3.

The first three months... That number! At Malta Bks was taken up with basic training. We all had to experience this period of brain washing. The instructors called it "preparation" for joining our given platoon but we all knew it was the period to make you forget all about having things done for you, like having your bed made, or washing and ironing your clothes or polishing your shoes. It was also a period to learn how to march, how to fire a rifle and kill people, what the army ranks were (important), how to address people with rank and how to salute.

And it was also the period to get us physically fit — miles and miles of road walk and runs and relentless hours in the gymnasium. The term "road walk and run" was totally inaccurate because we never, ever, walked. We started running and we kept running. If you slowed and fell behind during the company runs you were put in the "Duffers" squad when you eventually caught up, usually back at camp, and you had to immediately go out again for another thirty-minute run. I frequented the duffers squad on most road walk and runs. My rogue gene made sure that I was never as fit as the majority of the guys in my platoon, so I was never able to keep up.

So back to the number three. How was this number significant? Well, In all sorts of ways.

Whenever you mustered for "parade" you lined up in threes. You did this, initially, by forming a single line, tallest on the left and smallest on the right. Everyone then turns right and marches "into line", each soldier progressively taking up position in the front, centre or rear rank. There was an instructor "guiding" you in by bellowing, "FRONT," or, "CENTRE," or, "REAR!" in your ear as you passed him. Having done this once you were expected to remember your exact place in the platoon, forming up in precisely the same place each time you mustered for parade.

We learned that the number three featured in many other aspects of army life. Take coming to a halt, for instance.

On a macro level, when you were "drilling" in threes — that's practise marching in three lines, or ranks, for you non-military personnel — there was always one person picked out of the squad to give the commands. The idea here was to get everyone to do something all together. Right turn, left turn, about turn, etc. The commands always preceded an action that can be broken down into three moves. So, for example when the command "HALT" is bellowed at you the moves are as follows:

The command "HALT" is given as the left foot strikes the ground.

Each soldier then counts to three out loud as follows:

Everyone shouts, "CHECK" (this counts as one). The right foot strikes the ground in time. This is intended to slow you down.

All shout "23" (that's two and three in short, sharp steps, as in two, three and not twenty-three). At the same time the left foot then the right foot gets slammed into the paving in half the time you were marching. This is called "slamming your tabs in".

Try it at home: "HALT", "CHECK 23".

There you have it. Everyone comes to a halt and stands to attention as the drill instructor berates those that got it wrong or were the least fraction of a second out of time, or "NOT TOGETHER!"

An extension of this procedure is used when going up to and saluting an officer, as follows.

Slam your tabs in, as above, approximately three arm's length from the officer by marching towards him, then bellow

"HALT" to yourself inside your head! You must do this silently, in your head, because if you bellow it out loud at the officer's face, he might get a bit confused.

Standing to attention, you then inwardly count one, at the same time raising your right arm to the salute position, holding this position to the count of 23 (that's two, three, remember?) followed by "down" 23, smartly lowering your right arm back to the position of attention.

You can now speak.

So here's a quick precis of this.

March up to the officer and slam your tabs in. 23 [arm] up 23 [arm] down. Speak. Finished speaking? [arm] Up 23 [arm] down 23 about 23 turn 23, march away.

So 1, 23 1 gets used a lot.

Even when the Queen merits a "HURRAH" from the troops that's done in threes.

The parade Commander shouts, "READY… HEADDRESS!" The soldiers raise their right arms and grab the top of their caps

The parade Commander shouts, "HIPHIPHIP," that's "Hip" three times.

The soldiers inwardly count 23 at the same time grabbing their caps then, think "one", holding their caps with an outstretched arm, and shout, "Hoorah," at the same time, then think 23 before thinking "down" 23, smartly lowering their arms and holding their caps on the top of their heads.

The procedure from the command "HIPHIPHIP" is repeated twice more (that's three times in total) before the soldiers adjust their headdress properly.

The command "PARADE 'SHUN" is bellowed and the soldiers return to attention.

When the band is on parade and stood to attention, they raise their instruments to the count of three.

The Director of Music (DoM), or the Bandmaster (BM), smartly raises his baton and the band members inwardly count 23 then smartly raise their instruments into position, usually with music cards being thrown everywhere by the speed and force of the raising of instruments! It's a good idea to learn your part "off by heart" 'cos you can never, ever bend down to pick up your music, and you will never see this again, unless the DoM or BM picks it up for you.

There are many other times 1, 23 1 comes in handy but I'll not go into these. You army chaps will remember.

In conclusion, the moral here is;

If you can't count up to three DO NOT join the army.

CHAPTER 11
Bill's good deed.

August 1966.

Having joined the army at a really mature age of fifteen years old, I, and the other young soldiers like me, had to make friends fast. And we had to choose our friends carefully as we never knew when we were going to be knifed in the back by a "mate".

Being knifed in the back became a very strong and powerful asset to my rogue gene, but I'll not digress into this particular area of my momentous life at this stage.

We had just spent almost six months being weaned from our mother's apron strings and the army decided that we needed a rest from our routine of PT, education, music, weapons training, drill, more PT, etc... So it was time to go on leave. During this initial period of brainwashing — induction training they called it — I hooked up with a bloke who we'll call 'P'. Knowing that our summer leave was rapidly descending upon us 'P' and I decided to go stay at his parents' house for the first half of our three-month furlough.

On the day of our leave, we queued up for our pay and rail ticket and we were transported to the local rail station with three hundred pounds cash in our pockets and a rail ticket to the destination we had "requisitioned", in this case 'P's' home town of Hull. The money was paid in cash to us because we didn't have a bank account at that stage.

The cash we had was the result of the Army's way of teaching us the value of money. On a weekly basis we had to queue up for our ten shillings "pocket money", the rest of our wages (twelve pound fifty), having been held back to provide us with some spending money during leave periods. We were instructed that this was intended to pay rent to our parents for staying at home, to cover bed, board, heating and lighting. We all agreed to this, but I doubt that any of the boys paid their mums a penny. In any event, most of our parents didn't have heating as we know it now with radiators and the like. We got warm by sitting in front of a coal fire in the "front room". Only the rich kids had a lounge at home with their own fireplace in their own bedroom, but there weren't many rich kids in my intake.

Off me and 'P' went to Hull.

That summer we had a fantastic time going to the cinema, chatting up the girls, going fishing, visiting carnivals and chatting up more girls and generally doing the things that boys of our age did. Best leave period I ever had.

There is one particular event during that leave period that stands out for me.

'P' and I were in his back garden doing a bit of 'tidying up' for his mum. Weeding and tilling the soil in exchange for the bed, board, heating and lighting that we were enjoying. Chatting away we heard a sort of whimper. Standing up from our weeding we looked at each other and then saw 'P's' next door neighbour's daughter clutching her throat and bending almost double. This young girl looked to be about five or six years old and first impressions were that she was trying to be sick. 'P' shouted, "Are you OK?" The girl looked at us and we saw a ghastly sheet white face with vivid blue lips and eye sockets. It was abundantly clear that she was choking on something.

'P' and I were suddenly driven by the urge to get to her and we vaulted over the neighbour's fence and, trampling anything under foot, dashed to the girl. Not ever having had any medical training we were both at a loss as to what should be done, but we both instantaneously had a gut feeling that gravity was the best solution to rely on here, so we lifted the girl up and 'P' suspended her by her waist, pointing her head towards the ground. The girl, by this time was becoming limp and had stopped whimpering. Her hands and feet were also beginning to twitch and her lips had turned a darker blue!

I felt like a spare part as 'P' instinctively started to pump the girl up and down in an attempt to shake out the obstruction in her throat, to no avail. Then a thought occurred to me… "Let's see if I can loosen this obstruction by massaging her throat in the direction of her mouth." I told 'P' to keep pumping and I grabbed the girl's throat. The first thing I noticed was a hard, rock-like object roughly where I thought her Adam's apple should be. "That's not right," I thought, so I gave this object a squeeze and pushed it towards her mouth. Didn't work at first and the girl was now like a loose pile of washing in 'P's' arms. He continued to pump and I continued to massage with my left hand. With my right hand I gave her a mighty thump in the centre of her shoulder blades. That must have hurt, but she couldn't have noticed because by now she was clearly unconscious.

'P' then grabbed her feet and upended her. I continued to massage and thump and suddenly out dropped this "penny chew". You could buy penny chew's for… a penny. They were small slabs of nougat about the size of a pencil eraser. Pencil eraser? What's that you ask? Well, for those of you not old enough to remember real writing, with lines on the paper, you used a pencil eraser to rub out any mistakes you had made when writing with a pencil.

Anyway, we digress… Back to the girl.

When this sweet dropped out of her mouth she suddenly drew in an enormous breath. We laid her down and kneeled next to her until signs of life began to reappear. Although she was breathing heavily, as if she had just run a marathon, the colour in her face returned and she opened her eyes. 'P' and I were really relieved 'cos we had never seen an actual dead body before. All this took about two minutes, but it seemed more like two days.

Now, you might think, "Good job done, boys!" But my rogue gene decided otherwise. Notwithstanding the fact that we had just saved this girl's life some payback was merited for our good deed!

'P' and I heard something akin to a bull charging through a forest and Mr. Next-door-neighbour bellowed angrily, "Oi! GERROFF HER YOU FU****G BAS****S!" I think that he thought we were doing something sinister to the apple of his eye. Despite this guy's huge frame, he was quick. 'P' just managed to dodge his foot but my left temple took the full force of his size twelve. I went out like a busted light bulb. When I [eventually] woke up the first thing I saw were two faces. 'P's' mum and Mrs. Next-door-neighbour. 'P' and his mum helped me to my feet.

Standing about five yards away was Mr. Next-door-neighbour with the girl wrapping her arms around his leg. He looked just a bit sheepish.

Mrs. Next-door-neighbour said, "She told him what happened and he said he was sorry."

"I didn't hear him."

"No, you were unconscious at the time."

Does apologising to an unconscious guy count?

Mr. Next-door-neighbour said, "I saw you leaning over her touching her."

"We had to do something."

"What else did you do?"

"Nothing. She was choking!"

Now, some men (Yorkshiremen in particular) just cannot admit they are wrong and say 'sorry'. I guess it's a sign of weakness that they can't swallow. I sometimes have the same problem even now! So they have to find another way to say 'sorry'.

"That doesn't give you permission to trample all over my rhubarb."

'P' exclaimed, "We weren't thinking about saving your rhubarb. We were more concerned about saving her."

"Well, those rhubarb plants cost me two shillings and sixpence. You'll have to pay for them."

Now the idea here is for me and 'P' to offer to pay his two shillings and sixpence and then he would say, "No, it's okay. Thanks for what you did."

Me and 'P' looked at each other like we'd just snorted some white powder on a strange planet, but with three hundred pounds in our pockets I suppose we could afford two shillings and six pence.

'P' said, "NO CHANCE," and we both turned our backs on this guy and went indoors.

Mrs. Next-door-neighbour came round to 'P's' house

about an hour later and told us that we deserved a reward. I had this fleeting thought that perhaps my three hundred pounds was going to be augmented, but from behind her back she proudly produced two sticks of rock with 'Blackpool' through the middle.

She told us that she bought them in 1962 (it's now 1966) and she was keeping them for a 'special occasion'. We couldn't refuse, could we? After all, Mrs Next-door-neighbour looked so sincere and I suppose that this could have been a special occasion and it's the thought that counts.

That gift was about as close to a thank you as we would get, and I never received a proper apology for my brief unconscious state.

But what the hell? Me and my mate had just saved a girl's life!

CHAPTER 12
Bill's Skives

More often than not I preferred to sit in the practice room and hone my trombone skills, rather than doing PT, or going for a road walk and run, or washing the dixies in the cookhouse.

These distractions were unavoidable. PT and running was an integral part of one's military training. After all we were supposed to be fit in the army, weren't we? Everyone had to do it, regularly. Runs on Wednesday mornings at six a.m. The whole company. PT for the band on Friday, last thing at four thirty p.m.

Washing dixies was a task that nobody — and I mean nobody — wanted to do. "It was a dirty job but somebody had to do it," as the saying goes. But not the cook.

Explanatory Note:

Dixie n., pl. -s 1. The name given to dirty crockery and cutlery after use as implements to eat one's meal. 2. The name given to dirty pots and pans used to cook the ingredients that make up the meals that causes the crockery and cutlery to be dirty. 3. The name given to the tables and work surfaces on which the ingredients for cooking the meals, that make the pots and pans dirty, are prepared. 4. The name given to the floor on which the tables and worksurfaces, used to prepare the ingredients for cooking the meals that make the pots and pans dirty, stand.

In other words, scrubbing, washing, cleaning and drying the whole of the cookhouse and everything inside… Except the cook! He supervised and any pan that wasn't spotless was sent away to be cleaned properly.

The whole company of boys was placed on a roster and we had to do a stint in the cookhouse. We didn't have modern things like dishwashers or non-stick pans in those days. We were the dishwashers and we were provided with copious supplies of wire wool, paint scrapers, nail brushes, dish cloths and washing up soap.

All the physical stuff (PT, etc.) gave everyone a healthy appetite. Meals were woofed down and we rarely had time for seconds because there was always something to keep us busy until the next meal, or until lights out. And anyway, the dixies were removed from the hotplate to be taken to the washup area to be emptied, scrubbed, cleaned and dried immediately the last boy in the queue had been given his supply of mashed spud, gravy and anything else on display.

I have to say that we weren't exactly starved. The army always made sure that we had a good meal inside us, but it would have been nice to have had some more rice pudding, or chocolate sponge or even some bread and jam. However, working in the cookhouse gave me and a couple of my mates an idea.

Next time we had cookhouse duty somebody had to leave the storeroom window unlatched so that it could be opened from the outside. That night the guys in my billet got our heads down for 'bed check' and when we heard the clock in the clocktower above the company office chime eleven thirty p.m. we drew straws to see who would raid the cookhouse.

One of my mates drew the short straw and he got dressed

in his night gear for the raid. He even put cam-cream (camouflage cream) on his face in true Hollywood blockbuster fashion! After climbing out of the window — he could have gone out the door but that just didn't feel like a night raid — he pads across to the rear of the cookhouse and climbs through the window. The guards didn't do a very good job that night.

We all knew that inside the storeroom was an Aladdin's cave of goodies; tinned rice pudding, bars of chocolate, cakes, biscuits, pies, jam tarts. Everything one could imagine that would have made a feast to be proud of. What did he bring back? A tub of ice cream! I ask you, a tub of ice cream? What the hell could we make out of a tub of ice cream? He didn't even bring any wafers! He could have lifted some roasted chicken or a lump of cheese or some cooked ham or scotch eggs or even some bread and jam but what did he choose? Ice cream!

We got through about half the tub before we'd had enough and it had to be returned to the cookhouse.

*

Like I said, running was not my idea of enjoyment. I may have mentioned that more often than not I finished up in the duffer's squad after a run, so I had to do something to help me avoid running. PT wasn't so bad. I didn't mind swinging from ropes or doing somersaults over the horse, but running scored in the high minus one hundred by me and I hatched a simple plan to get some light duties. It was a gamble because I could have been placed on cookhouse duties — marginally less enjoyed than running — but perhaps my plan would render me unfit for even those tasks.

The plan:

Get a mate to punch you in the ribs hard enough to bruise them, then go sick with bruised ribs.

I had to choose a good mate. One that would not say anything afterwards. And one that was sufficiently intelligent to punch me with enough force to bruise my ribs, but not so hard that it caves the side of my rib cage in or collapses my lung or bursts my spleen. I approached a mate and discussed my project with him. He was agreeable... But then he would be because he enjoyed a good scrap, especially during 'murder ball'. I frequently saw him sneak the odd punch at some bloke in the opposing side when we were in a scrum.

I lifted my right arm and pointed to the precise place he should aim for. In true musician fashion we decided to have a rehearsal to get it right.

Thump!

No... I didn't mean thump now. THIS IS A REHEARSAL. You were just meant to practice your aim. And I wasn't ready for it!

"Okay. That's the correct place to land your punch," says I, "But it was not quite hard enough to hurt."

If it hurts, we know it will be a good punch. "Try again."

Whoomph!

A small intake of breath. Perhaps I should have taken a breath before that punch. We'll give it about half an hour then take a look at the bruise.

We had tea then went to the billet to inspect the impact site. What? Nothing! Not a thing! Not even a red mark? Perhaps bruises take longer to appear? Let's give it another half hour.

I finished preparing my kit for the following day which

took longer than the half hour we gave my bruise to surface. Still nothing. Okay. Maybe it needs a slightly harder punch? Not too much because I want to be able to play my trombone after it.

Now, my mate was beginning to get bored with this exercise and to be honest I was beginning to think it wasn't such a good idea anyway. After all I'm the one being punched and, in the normal course of events, I don't usually allow that to happen. But we'll give it just one more try.

He was not one for doing half a job and he had it in mind to embellish his punch by poking the knuckle of his middle finger in out front of the rest. I didn't know this primarily because I never saw it, primarily because he was stood to the right of my raised arm out of sight. Neither did he give me time to take a breath or say, "Now!" He just took an almighty bash and buried his fist into my rib cage.

WALLOP!

I froze. Not because I wanted to but because; a) I couldn't breathe and b) I couldn't move. The pain was excruciating. After about ten seconds I decided it was time to take a breath... The one I should have taken before the punch, and the pain in my ribcage just multiplied by two million percent. I had to ask my mate for help to get to my bed to sit on it.

Sitting on the bed I gingerly lifted my arm for inspection. Yep! There was the bruise we wanted. And it was a good one. A big one. He was pleased with the result but I had no thoughts about it one way or the other. I was concentrating more on breathing and trying to stay upright. It really hurt. But my discomfort confirmed the need to go sick tomorrow morning to get the Medical Officer's (MO) opinion.

After an uncomfortable night I queued up outside the

MO's office. My turn now and I heard the much-awaited word "Next!" Stiffly, I shuffled in and declined the MO's invitation to, "Sit!" I knew it would be a hell of a job to stand up again. The MO's assistant even had to help me take my shirt off. The MO looked, he prodded, he raised my right arm to an accompaniment of, "Ooooh," and, "Uuuuu," and he gave me a squeeze just underneath my armpits. I cried out in agony and the MO asked how I'd done this.

"Murder Ball," I answered.

He commented that he, "Must have a word with the PTI's (PT Instructors) about murder ball." He ordered a Land Rover to take me for an X-ray.

Explanatory Note:

Murder Ball n. a game where two teams compete and grapple on a small field to gain ownership of a medicine ball placed in the centre of the field and take this back to the victor's own goal. No holds barred and no rules, with everyone in the teams taking part in the mass scrum to own the medicine ball.

On return to the MO's office, with my X-rays in a sealed large brown envelope, he confirmed that I had three broken ribs.

The whole of my chest was strapped up with elasticated bandage. Really tight. And I was given three month's light duties to give my ribs time to heal. The purpose of this exercise was, therefore, a resounding success and, ultimately, worth the pain!

In fact, it was a success in more ways than one. It transpires that the MO had been seen by several of the boys after each game of murder ball, with injuries similar to mine… Maybe not as bad because all they had were small bruises!

Much to everyone's delight murder ball was banned for the foreseeable future. The PTI's were not too pleased because they saw murder ball as a toughening up exercise.

Word got out that I'd 'taken one' for the boys and I was secretly lauded for my pains.

This wasn't the only time one of my pals and I had the idea to evade work.

*

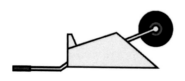 Being in a forested area autumn created a lot of problems with fallen leaves throughout the camp. They got everywhere. They polluted the square, a major transgression by the trees because the square was "for drilling on and not for producing a picturesque scene", according to the RSM.

Fallen leaves blew under the billets, a significant fire risk during the summer. They blew up against the company office and looked untidy and they made all the paths slippery and difficult to march on. They were a nuisance. So from September until all the leaves had abandoned their branches we joined a roster for 'sweeping the leaves'.

This wasn't a bad job. Not too taxing on the muscles, or brain if it came to that, and leaf-sweeping duties got us out of square bashing occasionally and even cookhouse duties. Our names were posted on Part One Orders for the following day and, when chosen, we had to report to the stores to draw out a wheelbarrow, a rake and a shovel. Our names were in teams of three... (There's that number again, see chapter 9 to remind you of the significance of the number three in the army.) In teams of three we had to work our way through the camp sweeping up leaves and taking them to the incinerator to be burnt with the rest of the camp's rubbish. And before you ask, yes, there was a roster for incinerator duties!

My mates and I preferred to skive off behind the gymnasium, smoke cigarettes and just sit there and chat. It was easy to occupy this place because we were "sweeping leaves" and nobody questioned our motives for heading towards the gym. It was nice and quiet. Tucked away and rarely visited by anyone in authority. At the end of our leaf duty, we could put a handful of leaves in the wheelbarrow, take them to the incinerator and then fall out. A nice easy day of it while the leaf-sweeping teams — including us, three to be precise — battled against the wind to pile up their leaves ready to shovel into their wheelbarrows ready to take to the incinerator, only to have their pile of leaves blown back to where they had started.

On arrival at our hidey-hole behind the gym my mate turned the barrow upside down and sat on it. We had a pleasant morning smoking, chatting and generally doing nothing of use, and we decided it was time for lunch.

Just as we stood up to leave our den, the Company Sergeant-Major (CSM) appeared round the corner of the gym, lighting a cigarette. He had obviously earmarked this hidey-hole as the place to go for a crafty smoke. And he obviously didn't expect anyone else to be there, judging by the surprised look on his face. He figured that attack was the best line of defence, considering he wasn't supposed to be there either.

"What are you three doing here?"

"Sweeping leaves, sir."

He looks, suspiciously, at our tools and turns his puzzled eyebrows to the upturned wheelbarrow.

"Why is that barrow upside down?"

There was a pregnant pause and my mate spoke up. Better to tell the truth in situations such as this.

"Well sir. If it was the right way up some f******g idiot would put something in it."

My other mate and I stood there, stunned. We waited for the torrent of abuse from the CSM that this audacious comment would surely provoke. What was in the back of my mate's mind, however, was that when questions were asked, and surely questions would be asked if charges were brought against us, the CSM would have to admit that he was skiving off, as well as ourselves.

After a long thought, either for effect or because he didn't know how to respond, the CSM quietly says, "That was an inspired answer, lad. It shows quick thinking and good leadership skills whilst under pressure. Now get off to lunch and don't let me catch you skiving again."

The CSM never mentioned his skive and we knew that we should not mention it, either, to anyone...

Twenty months of JPC, and I enjoyed every minute... Except for the runs and cookhouse duties. It was now time to grow up, become a man and join the men.

I was posted to The Royal Military School Of Music, Kneller Hall, Twickenham (RMSM), better known by army musicians as KH...

CHAPTER 13
Bill's Challenges

In September, 1967, I was posted to Kneller Hall (KH). I was just seventeen years old.

This posting was somewhat of a privilege posting for those musicians that were good at playing their instruments. Annually, a select few were given an opportunity to become pupils at the school and the selections were made from all the army's bands in Queen Elizabeth II's Commonwealth realms.

I never counted, but I guess that there must have been maybe three hundred musicians on the bandstand during our summer concerts, about one hundred of which were Student Bandmasters. These guys were the cream of the army's musicians, everyone on a three-year course to become bandmasters of their own bands throughout the British and Commonwealth armies.

Most army musicians aspired to be bandmasters, but only a select few were chosen. Pupils, like me, were on a twelve-month course to hone our skills on our instruments, with some music theory thrown in.

It was a sight to behold, three hundred musicians dressed in their regimental uniforms, or Number Ones as we called them, taking a seat on the open-air bandstand on a balmy night. And what a variety of uniforms from the Commonwealth countries. What a glorious sound it made. On the trombone line-up a student took up position of top trombone. I was placed immediately next to him by the professor who auditioned me on entry to the school. I was so proud to have been chosen for this prestigious position.

Something else we had to do, as soldiers, was to keep fit, so every Wednesday afternoon we had sports. The whole school congregated on the playing field to run, jump, chase, skip, hang, climb and carry out all manner of sports. It was mandatory. Those that didn't take part in any particular sport had to jog round the athletics track until it was time to go get a shower... usually two hours from the start. A couple of mates and I usually did two laps of the track then turned left towards the billets about five or six minutes from the start, depending on how energetic we felt. I can say, with all confidence, that rogue gene didn't like me running, either, because it gave him a rough ride while relaxing in my ball bag.

During the summer we had sports day when all four companies, A, B, C and D, competed against each other to see who was best at sports. There was no trophy, just points, and the company with most points won the competition. I was in D company.

Seeing as how I wasn't too keen on running, I tried to keep my head down when the company commander started choosing his team. Rogue gene, however, had other ideas! The company commander was an ex-para and he was keen to show off his regiment's prowess. From the ranks he chose all the para members and the final race to fill was the three miler. Inevitably I was the last para on the list, so I was it. The three-mile racer. What a bummer! Despite all the arguments, pleads and excuses put forward by me against this decision the guy stuck to his guns and flatly refused to put a Fusilier or a Tank

Regiment guy or a Scots Guard chap in for the three miler and I ended up taking my place on the starting line.

And guess what? I came last. Not surprising, really, in view of my rogue gene's efforts to keep me unfit.

Now, there was a Student in A company who was also an ex-para. He had passed his exams and was now waiting for his band. I remember him from the times JPC band was integrated with one Para to do a marching gig. I didn't like him then and I certainly hadn't changed my mind about him when I joined the school. He sidled up to me when I had finished my marathon — about five minutes behind everyone else — and spat venom in my face.

I was an embarrassment to the Regiment,

I was an embarrassment to JPC,

I was an embarrassment to KH,

I was an embarrassment to D company,

I was an embarrassment to all Paras,

I was an embarrassment to my red beret,

I was an embarrassment to the army,

I was an embarrassment to my company commander, and

I was an embarrassment to him.

In fact, "I've a good mind to take you round the back of the bandstand to give you a f*****g good thrashing!" he says, pointing his finger about half an inch from my face.

This was a challenge I just could not refuse. So I grabbed his sticking out finger and towed him behind the bandstand. On arrival I gave this odious little man an invitation... With conditions.

"You can have the first swing. I'll not even defend it. But after that... You... Are... Mine!"

He stared me in the face for about five seconds, then tried

to sucker me with a jab to my nose. Not good enough! I'd anticipated his move and just as he threw the punch, I moved my head sideways. He missed and smashed his fist into the wall of the bandstand. That must have hurt! While he's nursing his broken knuckles, I brought my knee up into his groin. That, also, must have hurt him... And probably his own rogue gene!

I decided not to take this any further and casually walked to the showers, leaving him on the floor gasping for breath and nursing his squashed scrotum. While taking a shower I thought to myself, "Well, that's my time finished at KH. I'll no doubt be posted back to my regiment in disgrace. Dropping a student is definitely jail time." Boy soldiers were definitely not permitted to assault a Warrant Officer 1st. Class!

But the guy never said a word. I've absolutely no idea what excuse he gave for his broken hand when he went sick, but he never let on about our little scuffle behind the bandstand. Perhaps he reflected on the fact that he initially threatened me. Or maybe he remembered that he took the first swing. Either way, the truth would come out and he would be in as much trouble as me...

*

During my time at KH I faced a much bigger challenge than defending myself against a prat. I met my future wife!

How?

The guys in my room frequently went out on the town and always came back with stories of their feminine conquests. Their favourite haunt was The Castle, at Richmond. At this venue there were two dancehalls, separated by the entrance foyer and bar. Ballroom dancing took place in the room on the right. The disco hall was on the left.

I, personally, had never danced so I knew that I couldn't dance and never would be able to dance. I still can't dance so I never try. Anyway, one Saturday night my room mates were all donning clean underpants and splashing after shave all over their freshly shaved faces, chests, armpits and anywhere else a friendly nose might survey. The room reeked like the perfume counter in a big department store.

One of the guys tried to persuade me to join them.

"Come on, Bill. Get dressed and have a night off."

"No thanks. I'm happy enough chatting up the NAAFI girls."

Explanatory Note:

NAAFI or Naafi (naffy) n 1. Navy, Army and Air Force Institutes. 2. A canteen or shop run by this organisation for military personnel.

"Come on. Forget the NAAFI girls and get your rags on. You'll have a great time."

"No. I've got things to do."

"What? Drink warm tea and twiddle your thumbs?"

"No. I've got some practising to get in before bed time."

"Come on. We'll pay!"

With that I could feel a slight shift towards splashing on some aftershave. One of the other guys nonchalantly mentioned that I was scared.

"No. Not scared. Don't want to."

"Yea. He's scared. He's scared to meet the girls."

"No. Not scared. I just don't—"

The guys grabbed me before I could finish my sentence, stripped all my clothes off, rummaged in my locker for a clean pair of underpants, dressed me, splashed aftershave all over my face and stood me up, all the time everyone laughing and jesting. So I agreed to go out on the town with them after firstly putting my underpants on the correct way round — they were inside out and back to front. Anyway, I didn't like being called scared.

Once inside The Castle we settled ourselves around a table in the disco side and one of the guys brought drinks to the table after taking the order. We sat there, chatting and joking as we eyed up the girls and they eyed us back. I didn't want to dance, 'cos I knew I was a rubbish dancer but the boys went off to home in on the girl that had the best... Eyes.

I was sat at our table guarding our empty glasses for a few dances. The boys eventually converged on me.

"Have you had a dance yet?"

"Nope. Can't dance."

"Yea. Okay. Look at him shiver with fear."

"Nope. Don't want to."

"He's scared."

"Not scared."

Now I knew that the boys could not attack me in the same way they did back at KH or they would be thrown out of the dancehall, so I stuck to my guns and just sat there while they tried to provoke me into dancing. Then I heard those provoking, confrontational words, "He daren't!"

I looked up at a wall of faces, all grinning and waiting for my response and knowing that I was not one to pass up on a challenge. I stuck my thumb out and pointed it over my shoulder. I hadn't even looked to see if anyone was behind me.

"See that bird behind me?" (That's what we called women back in those days.) "I'll ask her. Happy?"

"Yea, she'll do," the boys replied, grinning in agreement.

I stood up and turned round to see a young woman sat guarding some empty glasses. "Fancy a dance?" I ask nonchalantly, and expecting to be given a, "No thank you." That's how we asked women to dance back in those days.

That smile was a killer. She stood up and we walked towards the crowd, everyone gyrating to the pulse of the music. I looked back at the boys with a triumphant smile from ear to ear. No way were they going to call me chicken again. I made sure that we both buried ourselves into the centre of the pack so that we... I couldn't be seen making a prat of myself and suddenly the music stopped! With a look of surprise, we stood there as the DJ waffled on about something, and half the dancers were substituted by a fresh batch. She didn't even ask me to remove my hand from her waist.

After a couple of dances, I politely asked her if she would like a drink or a beverage of some sort. Actually, what I said was, "Fancy a drink?" 'cos that's how we asked women if they wanted a drink back in those days. My heart sank as she replied in the affirmative. Knowing the boys were going to pay I only had a couple of quid in my pocket, and back then the cost of drinks were a rip-off.

As we made our way to the bar, I was inwardly cursing my rogue gene. I was absolutely positive that he had constructed this corner that I'd backed myself into. Why did I have to show off? Why couldn't I have just bowed graciously and made my way back to my table full of empty glasses?

Plan B was to ask her to "hang on", then go and tap one of my mates for a couple of quid. When I saw her eyeing the optics, I knew I would need more than a couple of quid. The barman appeared in front of us with a grin as wide as the Grand Canyon. "Wotcha want?" he asks, looking at me. I turn to the woman and ask, gritting my teeth "What would you like?".

"A lemonade please."

Music to my ears. In the far corners of my mind, I heard the flourish of drums and the fanfare of trumpets. With luck I might even have enough change for a drink for myself. Yes, plenty of spare for a single scotch.

I picked up both drinks and we turned towards the disco hall. Being the gentleman that I was I let her go in front of me. Actually, it was nothing to do with being a gentleman, it was more to do with protecting our drinks from the comings and goings of the masses and seeing how good her legs were. We got as far as the steps leading down to the dance floor when she suddenly, without warning, put the brake on and stops dead in her tracks. I didn't see this coming and I almost ploughed into the back of her, applying my emergency brake. About a third of her glass of lemonade didn't stop but it shot forward and splashed onto the back of her dress. Bloody rogue gene!

However, she didn't give any indication that she had a wet patch on the back of her dress. She just moved into first gear again and carried on to her table of empty glasses. Was she just being polite? Did she even feel wet? Did she notice that a third of her drink was missing? Maybe she assumed I had drunk it? She never said a word. That showed just how considerate she was.

Anyway, she gave me her name and we sat and chatted the night away and made our drinks last for the remainder of the evening. I can't remember if we had any more dances.

When it was time to pack up the DJ said his goodbyes and powered down the turntables. The crowd shuffled outside and the woman and I stood on the top of the steps leading down to the pavement. From memory, I think she was the very first woman that I had not groped! I did, however, try for a kiss but all I got was a quick peck on the lips before she stood back.

I asked for her address. She gave me her telephone number. With that, I promised to phone and I joined my mates, waiting at the foot of the steps, to make our way back to KH.

Many years later she told me that she had seen me enter the room and stand looking onto the dance floor. That was obviously the time that my mates and I were carrying out our reconnoitre, having just arrived, but I don't recollect seeing her. She also told me that she fancied me, standing at the top of the stairs and that she had watched me and my mates take up position on the nearby table. After disclosing her phone number, she didn't hold out much faith in me 'phoning her for a date but she was wrong.

Women, back in those days, didn't make the first move. It was always up to the blokes to make the initial advances. That way the women could choose to say, "No thank you," or, "Get lost," or something else. But in this case, she wasn't going to say any of those things... She had her eye on me.

We've now been married for fifty-one years...

CHAPTER 14
Bill's Wings

"What manner of men are these who wear the red beret?

They are firstly, all volunteers and are then toughened by hard physical training. As a result, they have the infectious optimism and that offensive eagerness which comes from physical well-being. They have jumped from the air and by doing so have conquered fear. Their duty lies in the van of battle; they are proud of this honour and have never failed in any task. They have the highest standards in all things whether it is skills in battle or smartness in the execution of all peace time duties. They have shown themselves to be tenacious and determined in defence as they are courageous in attack. They are, in fact, men apart. Every man an Emperor. Of all the factors which make for success in battle the spirit of the warrior is the most decisive. That spirit will be found in full measure in the men who wear the Red Beret."

Field Marshal Bernard Law Montgomery, KG, GCB, DSO, PC, DL.

1st Viscount Montgomery of Alamein

 It is September, 1968. I had completed my training at KH and had been posted to my

114

parent band, the 1st. Bn. The Parachute Regiment... 1 Para. I was on top trombone.

I spent the Christmas period 1968/69 at my future wife's grandma's home in Harrogate. We got engaged. But all too soon I had to report back to Aldershot and I was taken to the station by a friend of the family.

News filtered down to 1 Para band that all three battalion bands were to combine during the following year to take part in a massed bands tattoo, touring the USA and Canada. This was an opportunity for the boffs in the MOD to show off its superiority of army music. But you cannot call yourself a parachutist if you haven't got your wings. So all those musicians who did not have wings, which by all accounts was every one of them, were given an order from on high to get them. As we were to have brand new uniforms tailor made for each of us, in time for the tattoo, it stood to reason the brand-new wings could be sewn onto these from the start. This would show everyone that we were, indeed, real parachutists and not, as the squaddies called us, "Penguins".

However, in order to qualify for wings training we had to be physically sculptured by attending a fitness course called 'P' Company (P Coy). We started P Coy in January, 1969. I ought to provide you with some explanation of P Coy; What it is, how long it takes, what's involved, etc... If this stuff bores you just skip over it!

Adult men (just men back in those days, no women) who want to join the Parachute Regiment direct from civvy street had to join the depot to undergo basic training. Once they join the recruitment programme, they lose almost everything; their identity, their dignity, their minds, their weight, their clothes and eventually, in some cases, their will to live.

The loss of everything required a bit of work by the army, and a lot of effort, heartache, tears, sweating and cursing by the recruits. Thirty weeks, non-stop, of physical torture by way of road runs and gym work, with a bit of rifle training and a lot of drilling on the square. It was extremely hard, physical stuff with PTI's bellowing how useless you were or how thick you were or how slow you were. The rest of the training, everything except physical stuff, was hammered into you by depot instructors, usually NCO's, who also bellowed how useless you were or how thick you were or how slow you were.

Anyway, if you were lucky to have survived that initial thirty-week brainwashing, during which time approximately half your intake had fallen by the wayside and been discharged, you then had to join P Coy for more physical restructuring of your body and mind.

This course was the worst possible nightmare of physical work one could ever imagine. In effect, it was the full thirty weeks of basic physical exercises squashed into two weeks! Unfortunately, for the band at least, this course was a compulsory requirement before continuing on to wings training. Only we didn't have the luxury of being nursed into this course by the thirty-week preparation!

At the end of this course, if you were lucky enough to reach the end, there were three specific tests to pass prior to being shipped out for wings training… Three? Again, that number! 1) the log race, 2) the stretcher race and 3) the trainasium.

The log race consisted of eight-man teams carrying a sixty-kilogram log over 1.9 kilometres while running. In our case the "log" was a telegraph pole. As if that wasn't enough to break ones back, the stretcher race was even worse! Sixteen-man teams carry a stretcher loaded with one hundred and seventy-five pounds over five miles, again running. Sheer torture, and if one person dropped to the floor during these races the team just carried on with one man short.

The last day of P Coy was dedicated to the Trainasium. This could only be described as a dangerous external gymnasium. There were ropes to climb, thirty feet tall. There was a "broken bridge", a single scaffold board hinged in the centre so that when you ran across this it suddenly tipped downwards as soon as you pass the half way point. This, again, was in excess of thirty feet in the air. There were the "shuffle bars". Two scaffold poles constructed horizontally atop an open scaffold tower well over thirty feet high. The horizontal bars were just over a body's width apart, about three feet, with scaffold clips attached to the these at intervals. One had to climb a rope to the top of the scaffold tower, shuffle across these bars and call out one's army number before lifting up a foot to negotiate over the scaffold clips. There was also a rope bridge; three ropes suspended high in the treetops, one to shuffle on and two at waist level to maintain one's balance.

We had to negotiate these things without any safety net. One slip and grab what you can, or splat! Call for an ambulance.

There were other life threatening pieces of equipment, such as fireman's poles to slide down... All thirty feet of the distance from top to bottom. Monkey bars over large patches of deep mud and ropes to swing across a trench about ten feet wide and just as deep.

The purpose of all this P Coy torment, torture, brutalisation and abuse was to "make a man of you", "instil some confidence" and "toughen you up". All the course did

117

was to transform you into a quivering mass of jelly. Pale, thin ghosts of men, good for nothing except a six-month furlough in a hospital bed, which we never got because we were "fit", and "tough".

At the end of P Coy we had to endure a psychological grilling by one of the course officers, a lieutenant. But this proved to be difficult for me to pass because my rogue gene decided to appear from wherever it had been hiding!

Prior to starting our fitness regime, we had to paint a unique number, provided by the course director, onto the left leg of our denim trousers. All this running through water and mud made the whitewash paint run, creating a long streak of indecipherable white staining with just the hint of a number visible. Unfortunately, my number twenty merged with the rest of the streaky paint down my leg and it became almost impossible to distinguish this from the number ten, the number given to a fellow bandsman that had refused the trainasium. I was judged to be psychologically unfit for parachuting by the course observer, notwithstanding that I had completed all the tasks meted out. I was gutted. Disappointment wasn't even near to what I felt and I was ready to explode with anger.

When the lieutenant informed me that I had failed, the first thing I did was silently curse my rogue gene. However, reading the paperwork over the lieutenant's shoulder while being given this shattering news, I noticed that he was referring to an assessment by the observer clearly giving the other guy's name.

"That's not my name," I protested, pointing at the assessment.

"Of course, it is," retorted the lieutenant, as if I didn't know my own name.

"It's not, sir. And that's not my number. I'm number twenty."

"What? No. We don't make mistakes like that," he says, trying to persuade me that he knew best.

"It's not! Number ten refused the Trainasium. I'm Number twenty... Pollard."

"Nooooo. Pollard passed."

"THAT WAS ME!" I pleaded, "Honest."

The lieutenant sat back in his chair and took a good long moment to come up with an idea to overcome this impasse. "Go and bring number six to me." With that his assistant left the office to find number six and return him to the interview room. On his arrival the lieutenant asked one question; "What's this soldier's name?"

"Pollard, sir. Number twenty," was the reply. He was given the all clear to fall out. After much tut-tutting the lieutenant gave me a long hard stare.

One last chance, I thought, to redeem this. "Please give me a break, sir. Give me a chance. I promise I won't let you down." After another long hard stare, he shuffles his papers to find number twenty's profile... My profile and he whacks it with his 'passed P Coy' stamp.

I couldn't thank him enough, despite his threat to, "Have my guts for garters," if I let him down.

What P Coy did do was make those of us who survived this gruelling punishment more confident. Confident enough, in fact, to take that huge step from an aircraft at two thousand five hundred feet with nothing more than a thin nylon canopy to slow our descent.

Almost immediately after our "passing out from P Coy" ceremony... Many of us passed out, all right, during P Coy!...

We were posted to RAF Abingdon for our wings training.

*

In comparison to what we had just been through this course was heaven. We were all extremely stiff for a while, but the stiffness was "rolled" out of us during three weeks of intensive parachute training. We learned how to "roll" when we landed. We learned how to jump with a container and we learned how to shuffle down the aircraft until we reached the exit door. We learned how to adjust the straps on our parachute, an important lesson in view of what my rogue gene had in store for me.

One of the training aids at Abingdon was given the name 'Knacker Cracker' by the instructors. This was a tall tower from which a zip wire was connected. Immediately below the exit doorway was a huge bundle of barbed wire. The idea here was to make you drive out of the door of the aircraft to overcome the slipstream that had a propensity to push you back into the plane. We didn't have the technology to simulate a slipstream back in those days, so the cheapest solution was to position this barbed wire so that you would get tangled in it, cut your legs to shreds and embarrassingly require help in extracting yourself... If you didn't drive out of the tower hard enough. Several of the guys finished up with their ankles covered in Elastoplast.

After our basic training we were ready to do this for real. Two balloon jumps and six from a Hercules troop carrier, two of these with containers.

I enjoyed every single jump, except one!

Parachute webbing (the straps) is designed to support you in two specific scenarios; a dry landing onto a DZ, or dropping zone, and a water landing into deep water. The webbing is attached directly to the rigging lines that are, in turn, attached to the canopy. One of these straps is horizontal and if one's webbing is adjusted properly this horizontal strap fits snuggly around the top of his legs where these meet his arse. Two more straps, attached to this arse strap, are pulled through your legs and attached to the quick release device located over your stomach.

Okay, all things being equal, you drive out of the aircraft and you are immediately stopped in mid-stream because the plane is travelling much faster than you. Your parachute is attached to a strop line inside the plane and the canopy, together with your rigging lines, is physically yanked from the pack attached to your body by the harness of webbing. It's like being hit by a steam roller travelling at two hundred miles per hour, and you ride the slipstream until the plane is well out of the way.

But with rogue gene involved all things are most definitely not equal!

The effect this sudden jolt to a stop has on your webbing is that all the slack in this is yanked tight in a split second. Think about it. If you haven't got your arse strap adjusted properly the only things stopping you from freefalling from a great height are the two straps that go between your legs. Arse strap too loose, it rides up your back. Legs straps then shoot up to your groin, trapping your reproductive parts between them... Your balls take the brunt of the two leg straps being compressed together in a fraction of a second and you have to suffer excruciating pain until your feet touches the ground and the pressure is taken off the straps. I suffered this on one of my jumps thanks to rogue gene, but only one. This taught me to adjust my webbing properly!

On almost every jump I made I heard some poor sod desperately screaming in agony as his arse strap shot up his back and his leg straps cracked together in his groin. You can hear it from about twenty miles away; "Aaaaaaaargh! HURRY Uuupppp!"

So, the "Knacker Cracker" was intended to teach us two important features of parachuting; drive out hard from the aircraft and make sure your harness is adjusted properly before take-off.

On the fourteenth February, 1969, we all passed out successfully from Abingdon and we made our way back to Aldershot to take up our instruments, once again, this time sporting our well-earned wings on our right shoulders.

We could now call ourselves Parachutists, equal to all the squaddies in the battalion who, by the way, gave the parachuting band members great respect for what they had achieved.

CHAPTER 15
Bill's Vow

March, 1969.

Having returned from Abingdon it took me, and the other guys who had endured P Coy, a while to return to full health. After a few weeks of decent grub, decent sleep and decent rest (i.e., No PT!) we all started to look human again. I turned out to be a real hunk. At least that's what I was told, but I'll let you make your own minds up.

Anyway, I was now engaged to my future wife and I vowed to restrict all carnal thoughts... And actions, to the shower. My rogue gene appeared to have gone dormant, so I got on with the serious business of being a musician.

During the summer months the bands and corps of drums rehearsed for The British Tournament and Tattoo, an overseas posting to the North America.

On the thirteenth of September we flew to New York courtesy of the British Overseas Aircraft Corporation (BOAC). Much to the pleasure of a couple of our guys the

BOAC air hostesses practiced their customer relations training on them behind the curtain dividing the seats from the galley. I know this because we had to go make our own coffee while the women were practicing.

For eleven weeks we travelled from New York to Ottawa, Canada, then all the way down the east coast of the USA from Montreal, across the bottom through Texas and New Mexico and up to Vancouver, Canada, calling in to eighteen cities to perform. Rogue gene had plenty of opportunity to make life interesting but he kept quiet for most of the time.

This gig consisted of four hundred and fifty plus army personnel from 1, 2 and 3 Para bands and corps of drums, bagpipes and drums from a Scots regiment, the Royal Signals Motorcycle Display Team, the RAF dog section and the Parachute Regiment gymnastic team containing a contingent of women from the Women's Royal Army Corp.

We travelled all this way in a fleet of Greyhound buses procured by the tournament's rich and famous producer. By the time we got to Vancouver my bus looked more like a hospital ward with all the pillows, sheets and blankets secreted out of our hotels.

The logistics of transporting and accommodating all these people plus instruments, drums, trampolines, motorcycles and a whole truck load of equipment must have been an organisational nightmare, but the tour passed without too many hiccups.

We performed at many of the prestigious venues; Huston Astrodome, where some guy flew a small aircraft around the inside. We must have looked like ants, from the seats way up in the gods. San Antonio, where the Alamo still stands. Tucson, Arizona, where many cowboy films were made. Los Angeles,

San Francisco, Seattle and many other notable places. Digital photography had not yet taken off so my suitcase was laden with thirty-five-millimetre film waiting to be processed by the time we arrived back in the UK.

From Vancouver we flew to Toronto, this time courtesy of the RAF and customer focused RAF air hostesses.

As rich as he was, the producer didn't exactly lash out on travel and accommodation arrangements. The Greyhound buses, for example, were the older models that didn't have a toilet so we had to make frequent stops to relieve ourselves of the copious amounts of booze that we drank. The driver of our bus was top drawer! He knew all the convenient places to call in to. Places that had a shop to purchase more booze and a toilet to get rid of the used booze.

Sleeping arrangements, also, were a bit derisory. In up market hotels,++ six guys were squashed into rooms that, ordinarily, accommodated two. Our rooms housing not one double bed but two double beds and two "put-you-up" camp beds. We also had suitcases, instruments and uniforms to cram in!

Now two men in the same bed was not what we were about and it was illegal in the UK army anyway, so we had to take turns to occupy either a bed or a put-you-up. If it was your turn for a bed, you overcame any embarrassment by either sleeping under the sheet or on top of the sheet. The same six guys shared the same rooms throughout the tour so we soon got into a good routine. From the outset we all agreed to keep our distance when in bed, especially after hearing the anticipated phrase, when bedding down for the night, "You touch my arse and you're a dead man!" God knows where the RAF dogs slept…

*

Our opening gig, in New York, was in Madison Square Gardens. Much to the chagrin of the NY police department a torrent of four hundred and fifty people, plus instruments, plus dogs, plus drums, plus bagpipes all diagonally flooded across the intersection of 8th Avenue and West 34th Street, holding up traffic in all four directions for about thirty minutes. On the first night a single traffic cop attempted to hold back this tsunami of bodies but we all know that it's impossible to prevent a tsunami from overwhelming the area it is engulfing, in this case the intersection. After a few abortive attempts he gave up. From the second night onwards, the intersection was saturated with cops and blue lights allowing the flood to drain unimpeded into the inner sanctum of Madison Square Gardens. The centre of New York, nonetheless, ground to a halt on performance nights, with a cacophony of cursing taxi drivers and blasting of car horns.

Everyone on the tour was perpetually surrounded by crowds of women of all ages, mums trying not to attract hubby's attention, a few blokes trying to attract the guy's attention, autograph hunters and salesmen trying to sell anything from legal services, pizzas and suspicious white powder to souvenirs and even women! Our hotel foyers were crowded with women in extremely short dresses — More like wide belts — men in short dresses, and taxi drivers, all offering to take us "sightseeing".

During one of the stop-overs I returned to the hotel room after a restaurant dinner to be faced with six or seven young women partying in our room. One of the lads had invited them up "for a drink". The beds had been stacked on the balcony, the radio was churning out songs and the girls were all dancing provocatively in their underwear. It was abundantly clear what everyone's intention was… Then I saw a pile of nun's habits draped over a chair!

One of the guys confirmed that they were not actresses paid to embarrass us, as in a birthday surprise. They really were nuns, out for "a quiet evening at the theatre". They had, apparently, been encountered by the blokes crossing with the tsunami and had been invited up to the room for a party after the show. Once inside the room the women turned into animals, then turned on the blokes who absolutely could not refuse such attention.

Surveying this scene, several thoughts collided with the back of my eyeballs; would I be able to face my fiancée when I got home? Would I even tell her? Who's going to know? Why the hell did I have to go and get engaged? Anyway, I was a rubbish dancer.

Silently cursing all sorts of words too obscene to print I reversed back into the corridor, closed the door and returned to the foyer. Our bus driver was an all-round good guy who appreciated that a person might prefer a bit of "privacy" occasionally. So he left the bus door unlocked for this very reason.

That night I slept on the back seat.

*

As the tour convoy made its way towards the west coast from Tucson, we had to cross the Arizona desert, bordering the state of New Mexico in the U.S. and Mexico in South America. This trip was a long, hot, boring drive with little to see except sand and cacti. There was no road, just a dirt track with patterns reminiscent of the infrequent vehicles that passed this way. There was nothing to do except play cards or catch up on some sleep.

After about an hour our bus slowed to a halt. The driver asked us for some help and we all vacated the bus to see what help was needed. We witnessed a spectacle that must have been rare in such a vast space.

There had been a head-on crash between two cars! How could that have happened? With no roads and hundreds of square miles for people to drive why had these two cars seemingly aimed at each other? Couldn't one of them get out of the way? I guess that both drivers' rogue genes had somehow telepathically communicated with each other!

Although both cars were steaming write-offs there were few injuries with the women sat on the ground tending their cuts and bruises.

Two men had decided that verbal intercourse at five paces was required and they stood at the side of their vehicles angrily pointing index fingers at each other, each blaming the other for, "Not looking where you were going," or, "Driving with your eyes shut."

There was absolutely no chance that their threats would be acted out because both men just didn't want to take their finger pointing to the next level. Nonetheless, a few of our chaps got in the middle of this verbal contest and separated the men who then joined their families whilst shouting derisory comments at each other. Once separated their bravery emboldened them to declare what they would have done if we hadn't have happened along…

The families took up our offer to take them to our next stop, San Diego, and we all boarded our buses for the next leg of this journey. On the way we stopped at a convenience store in the middle of nowhere. Here was a chance to stretch our legs, replenish our booze, empty out our used booze and buy some snacks and souvenirs.

Surprisingly, I noticed the two men from the car accident standing next to the bus chatting away, laughing, joking and acting as if they were lifelong friends.

People are really strange, sometimes.

*

After our gigs in San Diego, we loaded the buses and settled down for the journey to Long Beach, California. On arrival we checked into our hotel. We had a couple of days to relax and do some sightseeing before our next gig and that's just what I intended to do.

Early next morning one of our guys collared me in the hotel foyer to tell me that one of the senior NCO's, a sergeant, was looking for me. Pointing me in the direction of the bar I went to see what I was wanted for. Standing in the centre of the room the sergeant was chatting to a guy, his wife and their young son. Introductions over I entered into a conversation about the son's trombone playing. The mother suggested that perhaps I could give junior a lesson? The guy then proffered an invitation to take me on a tour of his Hollywood radio station, followed by dinner that evening and a bed for the night at his place. I graciously accepted his offer, thinking a home cooked meal was probably a respite from the stodgy hotel grub.

After a couple of drinks, we trooped out to his limo, patiently waiting outside the hotel. The driver opened the door and the boy got in, I got in, the wife followed me and the husband brought up the rear. Squashed between the boy and his mum I couldn't help thinking that she had a great pair of legs. As I sat there with my knees squashed together, the mum turned slightly towards me to provide a little more room. With her breast pressed against my arm and our knees fused together I found it difficult to hold an intelligent conversation with the dad, sat in the front seat. Anyway, I put this awkward situation down to the circumstances of the limo's size and looked forward to the tour of the studios, a decent meal and a comfortable bed.

The tour round the radio studios was fantastic. One of the DJs suggested to the dad that as they were on air it would be a good time to interview me and advertise the tattoo. With a shrug I asked if that would cost a lot, but the dad insisted it was good thinking on the part of the DJ. So I was microphoned up and sat in a booth opposite the DJ and I got interviewed live on Hollywood radio! Afterwards, the dad congratulated me and the DJ on an interesting, informative and humorous interview and he took us all out for a meal.

During the meal the dad and the DJ discussed work, mainly about how the studio could link up to the tattoo venue for a live concert, who they should contact for the rights and how much they should charge. It was agreed that the dad should return to the studio that night to initiate their plan.

The son and I discussed the inner workings of trombone harmonics, lip tension, slide positions, breath control and how the choice of mouthpiece influenced one's range of notes. He seemed fairly knowledgeable on all these subjects but he still made notes in a notebook that appeared out of his pocket.

His mum just sat there impassively taking it all in and, to my discomfort, exposing a lot of her legs!

After the meal we again trooped out to the waiting limo. This time I wasn't going to get tortured with the pressing of the bosom and joining of knees and in true gentlemanly fashion I ushered the mum into the car before me. Our knees still fused together but with me at a slight angle, this time, I could stay well away from the mum's assets. However, when the driver had to brake hard to avoid some idiot that had cut across the freeway lane, she steadied herself using my thigh as a support. When the driver accelerated, she sat back and her hand ever so gently slid off my thigh. As the driver was being admonished by Dad for his clumsy driving I was thinking, "Is she hitting on me?"

Spoiler alert! Rogue gene has woken up and is on the prowl for something to upset!

As soon as we arrived at the family's palatial pile back in Long Beach the dad poured me a drink then exited the house to return to work. Mum showed me to my room, making a point of showing off the voice activated lights and ordering the curtains to close by themselves. Junior poked his head into the room and just as he started to talk trombone, Mum ushered him back to his own bedroom with instructions to, "Put your trombone away for the night, clean your teeth and shout me when you are ready for bed." A bit disgruntled that he couldn't chat with me some more he slinked off to do as he was told. The mum and I went back downstairs to finish our nightcaps.

With junior well and truly tucked in the mum returned to the lounge for another chat and at about ten thirty p.m. I made appropriate noises that it was time I was in bed. I stood up, collected the glasses and took them to the kitchen. After carefully washing them and placing them on the sink drainer I returned to the lounge. The mum wasn't there. I looked in the reception room. She wasn't there either so I made towards the stairs, thinking that perhaps Mum had already decided to go to bed. She had... But not in the bed I expected!

At the top of the stairs, just outside my bedroom, the mum appears from hers wearing nothing but a flimsy dressing gown. How flimsy? At least ninety percent see-through. How did I know this? For a start, I could see the outline of her breasts, her nipples trying to force their way through the thin cloth, and I silently marvelled at her slender body. She said something about turning my bed down but I didn't really hear this. I was more interested in admiring her figure as she glided towards me. Stood in the doorway of my room my mind was awash with visions of what was about to happen but I couldn't move. I was paralysed from the neck down. My heart pounded to escape from my chest as it pumped adrenalin around my body and I felt the swell of testosterone straining against my trousers.

Mum placed her hands on my shoulders as she squeezed past me into the room. Her dressing gown caught on my shirt and opened to expose the full length of her beautiful form. My hand cupped her breast as she gave me a gentle lasting kiss. What else could I do? It was there, just begging to be fondled. She released the pressure from my trousers by lowering my zip. As we kissed, she gently squeezed my manliness and teased this with slow, stroking actions.

We both enjoyed each other's probes and teases for a few minutes. Actually, it was more than a few minutes... Before she made her way to my bed, dropping the dressing gown to the floor on the way. Lowering herself onto the bed she struck up an enticing posture as she smiled and said, "Well? Don't just stand there. Come and help yourself."

Then what happened?

Just as I'm wrestling with my shoes and trousers, we hear a plaintive cry from junior's bedroom. "Mum?"

She tutted and replaced her dressing gown, leaving the room to go see what the problem was with junior. I got into bed thinking, "What are you doing?" feeling a little guilty as to why I had not put a halt to this earlier.

When the mum returned to the bedroom about half an hour later, I could see that she, also, felt a bit guilty. I tried to put her mind at rest by saying that I couldn't do it as I was getting married in the new year and it wasn't fair to my fiancée.

Sitting on the edge of my bed she gave a resigning sigh and allowed me to have one last extremely lengthy grope... And another extremely lengthy probe while she gave me another extremely lengthy kiss, and then she left the room.

I laid in bed thinking what a prat I was to have passed up on what would have been a fantastic time. I'd better not tell the boys about it or I'll be demoted to the rank of imbecile. Then I realised that this little soirée was probably engineered by my rogue gene. To trap me. To embarrass me. To make me feel guilty. To test me.

But I had vowed to be good on this trip...

CHAPTER 16
Bill's Faux Pas

Have you ever said something in all innocence and then felt the ground open up below you? I bet you have. Most people have, but what you might not realise is that this faux pas is your rogue gene's way of having a laugh. You may not think so, but it's entitled to some light relief occasionally, isn't it?

I think you know, by now, that Yorkshire is the centre of the universe. Anyway, being born and brought up in Yorkshire I have made many innocent gaffes that have sometimes caused indescribable trouble for me.

Now these gaffes were undoubtedly influenced by the unique phonological dialect triggered by Yorkshire speak. The Yorkshire language is complicated. Yorkshiremen say things that, to others, mean something else. Take 'lamp' for example. I say 'lamp' to you and you think I'm talking about something that shines a light. Not so for Yorkshiremen. When they say "'lamp' their meaning is to strike or hit, as in, "You've offended me so I'm gonna lamp you reet ont' nose!"

Now there's a couple of odd words; "reet" is "right", and "ont'" is "on the". See? It's easy to understand when you can speak the lingo.

To make matters worse, Yorkshiremen tend to string this abbreviated slang together to make whole sentences! I'm sure you must have heard the phrase "t'in't in't tin". No? Okay, this means, "It isn't in the tin". We... Yorkshiremen, that is have even had songs composed with our unique slang words; "Ba'ht", meaning "without", as in "On Ilkey Moor bah't at" (without a hat).

We also give material things, things of substance, ludicrous names to confuse non-Yorkshire speaking people. Names like 'Goosegogs', meaning gooseberries, or 'Wasak', meaning useless person or idiot. "You've just stacked all those crates of goosegogs on top of that box of eggs. You're a Wasak!"

So, what has all this got to do with my faux pas? Let me explain.

At each of the stop-overs on our North American tour there was always an array of stands scattered around the arena selling food and drink. I loved those pizzas. Hot, tasty and ideal for the intermissions. At one of the stands, I approached the vendor and in true Yorkshire speak asked, "Have you got any fags?" Obviously, fags in Yorkshire speak means something entirely different in the USA! But I didn't cotton on... And neither did the vendor!

"You want what?"

"Some fags, please."

"How many?" looking at me with a look of puzzlement across his eyebrows.

"Just one packet."

"Just one packet?" eyes widening.

"That's all, thanks. I don't think I've got enough change on me for any more."

It may be of some use to you to know that back in those days (1969) it was illegal to advertise the fact that you were not shall we say... straight?

"You don't have enough money for more than one packet," this being said more as a statement of fact than as a question.

"That's right. Have you got any?" thinking I should be getting back to the line-up for the next half of the show.

"Are you sure you want some fags?"

"That's what I asked for… I've only got three left."

I'm thinking, "What is the matter with this bloke?"

"Just a minute," says the vendor and leaves his stall to disappear into the crowd.

Now I thought he went to get some packets of fags. In reality he returned with a cop!

Clearly, my uniform gave way to the fact that I was a Brit who was in the show. Hands on his hips, the cop asks me, "What is it that you want?"

Puzzled by this attention, and with a small crowd gathering behind us, I answered, "A packet of fags."

"Are you serious?"

"Yes, of course."

The cop looked at the vendor, looked at me, looked back at the vendor and reached behind his back for the handcuffs.

Fortunately, in the now fairly large crowd a Brit in uniform being part of the show, and a cop, wielding handcuffs attracts more attention than most people really want. In the large crowd was an ex-pat Brit who was enjoying the show. Not only that, he was a Yorkshiremen who knew exactly what I wanted.

Laughing, the ex-pat stuck his hand in between the cop and myself and explained that, "Where he comes from, in Yorkshire, England, fags is the name given to cigarettes!"

With a look of bewilderment on the cop's face, a look of

perplexity on mine and a look of recognition on the vendor's face, the cop replaces his handcuffs and whispers, "If you're going to come to the USA, you should learn to speak proper [sic]."

The crowd gave a mumble of amusement and dispersed, the vendor didn't have any fags and I sheepishly returned to the band assembling with instruments to begin the second half of the show. Better not let on to the guys what just happened. They might think I'm a wasak...

*

My rogue gene again prompted me to make a different kind of faux pas at a later show venue.

During a different interval, in a different venue, we were swamped with autograph seekers, flirting college girls, instrument players, ex-pats and people who just wanted to chat about nothing in particular. Three trombone players from the show and three civvies with trombones met, purely by coincidence, on a balcony overlooking the auditorium and decided, just for the fun of it, to play Frère Jacques. We soon amassed an audience, laughing, clapping and generally egging us on.

At the end of our impromptu performance a couple of women, one of which was well endowed with huge assets, approached us for a chat. They both sported unusual pullovers. One was a glitzy shiny thing with semi-hanging discs, arranged in the words "Bats do it". One of the guys asked what that was about and the women brushed her hand over the discs, reversing them to read "upside down". She even allowed my mate to brush his hand up and down her front to expose the words in both directions, although I suspect he wasn't too interested in the words!

The other woman, the well-endowed one, was wearing a long-haired jumper with the picture of a cat woven into the long strands of hair. My other mate reaches out and gently holds some of the hairs between his thumb and fingers and jokes that the cat must take a lot to maintain. No problem at all. We even joked that it must please the cat when the woman spilled food down her front. Still no problem.

The woman mentioned that she loved her cat and purely in jest — honestly, no, really — purely in jest I asked, "Can I stroke it?" I genuinely didn't want to stroke it. It was meant to generate a laugh. Instead, slap! Her right hand right across the left side of my face. Immediately after this slap her friend decided to join in and slap! Her left hand right across the right side of my face.

The guys split their sides laughing.

With my face feeling like it had been badly sunburned I thought to myself, "These Americans are difficult to predict." Bloody rogue gene must be really congratulating itself with this victory!

*

On yet another occasion I remembered my faux pas with the "fags" and thought I would box clever by asking for some fags by name. Up yours, rogue gene! You'll not catch me out with that mistake again.

The convoy, once more, stopped in the middle of nowhere. Just miles and miles of wasteland between San Francisco and Medford, our next venue. Nothing, as far as you could see, except a convenience store. This convenience store was hardly convenient. The size of a garden shed, the only stuff on display were cans of Coke and root beer. We had stopped there for the toilet, a single toilet, which suddenly had a queue stretching back hundreds of yards as the guys waited to get inside.

Luckily, I was one of the first to empty out my used booze and I went into the shop to buy some cigarettes. Approaching the counter, I ask "Have you got any Camels?" Camels are a well-known brand of cigarette in the U.S. and one would have thought that the guy with no neck, a broken nose and arms like the legs of a grand piano would know what I meant.

Don't forget that this is in the middle of a desert. Also, a couple of the guys had already exposed their English accent before I got there.

"We don't have Camels in this country," he says.

"Yes, you do. I bought some a few days ago."

"Uh? You did?"

"Yep," note the mickey-taking American accent.

"Camels."

"Yep, Camels."

"Where did you buy these Camels?" an enquiring look on his face.

"From a shop in San Francisco."

"And where are these camels now?"

"I've used them up," exasperation creeping into my voice.

"You've used them," a resigned tone to his voice.

"YES. Have you got any?"

He reaches below the counter and pulls out a baseball bat! "What are you? A nut job or what? Do you take me for an idiot?" wielding the baseball bat about ten inches from my nose.

I curtailed my desire to correct his vocabulary to point out that what he really meant was, "Do you take me for a wasak?"

Neither of us knew what each of us was talking about. I really didn't like the menacing look on his face and decided that discretion was, perhaps, the better part of valour. I backed out of the hut holding my hands up in submission.

This bloody rogue gene never stops, does it?

Waiting to board the bus my mate asks me, "Why is that guy telling everyone you're a nut job?"

"Don't know…"

CHAPTER 17
Bill's Time Travel

It's amazing what you can do when writing a book.

One of the things you can do is time travel, missing out whole periods of your life and continuing years ahead of where you last left off.

Our North American tour finished on the twenty-sixth of October, 1969. I'm now going to continue from May, 1972.

"What's happened to the period between October, 1969 and May, 1972?" I hear you ask. Well, I went to see a man about a dog.

Now, if you can't remember what I mean by that you must be a wasak! Refresh your memory by re-reading chapter 16.

One thing I can tell you is that during this period the battalion had been relocated to Mons Bks, on the outskirts of Aldershot.

And I got married on the fourth of April, 1970.

I must have been mad. No more flirting. No more gropes... With strangers, anyway. Whilst I might be ambushed in the future, I took my vows seriously and looked to settling down. Couldn't complain, though, 'cos my wife was, and still is, gorgeous. Even after almost fifty-two years of marriage.

Gorgeous, that is, until she starts to snore while I'm trying to sleep!

CHAPTER 18
Bill's Plan

In May, 1972, the band settled into its new home in Mons Bks and we resumed our annual round of carnivals and concerts.

From the time that I first joined the army in 1966 I had dreamt of becoming a conductor. This meant becoming a bandmaster, with the rank of WO1 (Warrant Officer First Class). This rank is just one step short of becoming an officer and a Director of Music (DoM). But I had to improve my prowess for music theory and my conducting skills before I could even think about reaching these heights.

I had to have a plan.

I decided to concentrate on the theory and at my own expense I commenced a correspondence course in Military Bandmastership. This was an open-ended course provided by a chap who lived in Deal, Kent. It covered all aspects of music theory, harmony and arranging for military band.

My plan was to learn enough theory to be able to pass the Royal College of Music's Associate's exam (ARCM) in Military Bandmastership. Naively, perhaps stupidly, I thought that if I could get this qualification then I would definitely be favoured for a place at Kneller Hall as a Student Bandmaster. I'll explain why in a moment, but this foolish notion was unwise from the start. I didn't even need rogue gene to interfere! But I was young and ambitious and didn't think this plan out to its logical conclusion.

After several years of a correspondence course my tutor suggested that I was knowledgeable enough to attempt the exam, providing I was proficient at conducting. Now conducting was a subject that I had put on hold until I knew sufficient amount of theory. But now was the time to start my conductor training and my own bandmaster (BM) gave me his valuable time, patience and, indeed, the use of the band to learn and practise my conducting skills. I submitted my exam entry papers and was given a future date for attending the college in London to take the exam.

I poured over previous exam papers and band scores during the evenings, almost every waking hour taken up with cramming as much in before the exam. I had been provided with the itinerary for the exam, together with a list of scores from which the examiner would choose for me to conduct on the day. I discussed the list with my BM and he suggested that it would be good for me to conduct a band different to my own. The Royal Corp of Transport (RCT) band was stationed just across the road from Mons, so I approached the DoM for an interview and went to chat with him a few days later.

I discussed my forthcoming exam with the DoM and asked if I could borrow his band. "Absolutely no problem," he says and we arranged a couple of days when I could return to practice conducting on his band. He, also, contributed his valuable time to teach me some skills and the band members were all co-operative during rehearsals.

Now I've just mentioned two guys that could have dissuaded me from taking this exam, for a very important reason, but they didn't and they should have.

On the eleventh of December, 1972, I travelled to London

for a gruelling three-day exam.

Day One — a.m. at the college of music, a three-hour theory exam. In the afternoon a three-hour harmony exam covering fugue, canon and three-, four-, and five-part harmony.

Day Two — a.m. at the college of music, a three-hour exam on the types and compass (range of notes) of the instruments in the military band, with a written discussion on what instruments make the best solos. In the afternoon a three-hour arranging exam, arranging for the military band from an orchestral score.

Day Three — a.m. at Wellington Bks in London, the home of The Welsh Guards at the time, to be tested on my practical skills. Three tests in all; perform a solo of my choice on my own instrument (I had to take my trombone) with the band accompanying me; a viva voce exam where I sat at a piano while a college examiner played chords that I had to name; and a note pitch exam where I was played two notes on the piano and I had to say what notes they were and what the interval was between them. In the afternoon was my conducting exam, rehearsing the band with one of the pieces on the list, followed by conducting of another piece. I had to rehearse The Sorcerer's Apprentice, by Dukas, and conduct from start to finish, non-stop, Jupiter from The Planets Suite by Holst.

At the end of the third day, I was interviewed by the DoM of the Welsh Guards.

Here's where I explain why I was a fool to take this exam, and why my BM and the RCT's DoM should have warned me of the risks in following this path.

When I took the exam, I was a mere private in the army. A nobody, with little experience of army life and with even less experience of managing men. I was destined not to pass this exam at this time for reasons that would only become apparent to me several years later.

The pass rate for the exam was, at that time, seventy-five out of one hundred. When my exam results eventually arrived, I eagerly tore open the envelope to see if I'd been successful. I had been awarded a mark of seventy-one. So near, yet so far away! I was gutted. My initial response was one of, "Thanks, Bill, for your one-hundred-pound exam fee. Come back next year with another one hundred pounds."

I initially blamed my rogue gene, but what I didn't appreciate was that I had, in fact, put the Welsh Guards DoM in an impossible position.

The crux of the matter is that the ARCM exam was taken by the KH Students <u>after</u> they had finished their passing out exam from KH, just prior to being promoted and posted as a Bandmaster. From my interview with the DoM he knew that if I passed the ARCM I could never go to KH as a student. How would it look to the other students?

So, the choices he had was for me to pass the ARCM and never have the opportunity to go to KH, or fail the exam and be in with a chance of becoming a bandmaster. A rock or a hard place!

In actual fact, in a perverse sort of way, he was trying to do me a favour by failing me the ARCM exam.

At the time I didn't realise just how much this incident would impact on my career…

CHAPTER 19
Bill's Light Duties

April, 1973, and it was time to pack up our instruments and board the RAF's plane again, with a new crew of "practising" air hostesses, for another tour. This time to Bermuda for a period of one month. The whole battalion went.

An advance party had been sent there two weeks prior to the rest of us to get everything ready for the arrival of the main party. The bandmaster (BM) and a band sergeant had volunteered to be the band's rep on the advance party.

When we arrived at our camp, we found that the advance party, as usual, had done nothing for the lower ranks of the band. Not surprisingly senior NCO's, sergeants and above, had nice comfortable accommodation. Lovely soft mattresses with clean sheets, blankets, pillows and pillow cases.

The unimportant ones (us) had to sleep on the bare bed springs. No sheets, no blankets, no pillows, no pillow cases. We had to use our towel for a pillow and we slept under our uniforms. Fortunately, the nights were pleasantly warm, probably much to the disappointment of my rogue gene.

If you have ever watched a military band marching and

playing at the same time you will have noticed the guy out in front with a large mace. He has the title of Drum Major, or "Drummy". Don't be fooled by this title. He's not a major. The title is an appointment, not a rank, but most drummies are sergeants, colour sergeants or WOII's (Warrant Officer 2nd Class).

The mace was used to signal a command to the band to do something; start, stop, turn, counter march, etc. Drummy also used his free hand to augment the mace commands; forward or turn for example. Our drummy, at the time, was vertically challenged so we couldn't see any of his hand commands. Only the front row of drummers, were lucky enough to see these so most of the time the rest of us just had to guess what was happening.

Now, many short men in the army had an attitude. They had to adopt this attitude from day one to stop taller men from taking the mickey. Our drummy had a real attitude. An attitude and a half even. This was intensified, somewhat, by his rank. He must have persuaded himself that the appointment of Drum Major actually gave him the privileges associated with those of a real major, because he strutted around barking orders at anyone in sight.

One morning the band was due to rehearse with the drums for a battalion march through the streets of Bermuda. This was the colonel's way of showing these Americans how it should be done. Anyway, drummy enters our billet and barks the order, "Shirts off!" I wondered if my rogue gene was setting me up for something bad.

Advisory note one — Even at that time it was illegal, in the army, to create self-inflicted wounds. Getting sunburnt by sunbathing was, therefore, a punishable offence.

Advisory note two — Having fair hair and fair skin I was almost guaranteed to burn in the sun without firstly getting acclimatised. We had been in Bermuda for just a couple of days so the chances that I was, by now, acclimatised were extremely slim. I was definitely going to get burnt!

I decided to approach this problem from a diplomatic viewpoint.

"May I keep my shirt on to stop me getting sunburnt, sir?"

"No! Shirts off!"

"But sir, I'll burn without some cover."

"So what? I said SHIRTS OFF!"

I really didn't want the possibility of being reported for self-inflicting wounds so, as calmly as possible, I replied, "Sir, are you going to explain to the company commander why I'm sunburnt, or shall I?"

"What? Are you stupid, or what? I've just told you to get your shirt off. NOW GET IT OFF!"

"Okay. Have it your way. I'm beginning to wonder which one of us is stupid."

"You're definitely on a charge for that. Insubordination!"

"Yea, yea!" I retort, then shout out to the rest of the guys in the billet, "Be careful where you walk. You might trample on the Drum Major by mistake on your way out!" making a reference to his challenged height. Much guffaw and laughter followed.

"GET OUTSIDE! EVERYBODY, GET OUTSIDE! I'll see to you later, Pollard. Don't think you've got away with this."

"Yea, Okay… Sir!"

Guess what? I got burnt. Really burnt. Badly burnt. The M.O. inspected my neck, back and chest and put me on light duties until my skin improved. He wasn't pleased. His parting words were, "I'll have a word with the Drum Major about this! If you see him first send him to me."

The M.O. put me before the Company Commander. It was mandatory for self-inflicted wounds. When I went before the major… A real major, he was ready to fine me but I interrupted his flow and made him aware that I hadn't inflicted these wounds personally. "The Drum Major ordered all of us to take our shirts off, despite my warning him about getting burnt." The major wasn't pleased, either.

He says, "I'll have a word with the Drum Major about this. If you see him first send him to me."

I didn't hear anything from Drummy about my charge… Nor did I have the pleasure of seeing him to let him know that the M.O. and Company Commander wanted a word.

My skin was so badly burnt that, many years later, I still suffer from repetitive bouts of skin cancer!

*

The PTI's proposed a road walk and run every other day through the streets whilst on this tour, a proposal endorsed by the colonel because it showed these Americans how fit we were… Even the band. Being a shrewd, and knowledgeable battalion commander, he knew that the band was fit for nothing, other than blowing instruments, so the order was given that there were not to be any duffer's squads during these runs. This was to show these Americans that everyone was super fit, with no exceptions. As a consequence of this order, we all had to run at a pace to match the weakest runner, usually myself and about three or four other bandsmen. The runs were deceptively slow but impressive, 'cos the duffers set the pace and the battalion was all counted out, and all counted in, together in threes... Yep, that number again.

The runs culminated in a mass disorganised charge by the whole battalion down the beach into the surf. At that time of the morning the surf was freezing cold so I had to think of a way to avoid both the runs and the freezing cold surf.

Now, if you get light duties you're excused silly games, like PT and road walk and runs. You still had to carry out your other normal duties which, in the band's case, was band practice. How could I get on light duties without too much trouble? I didn't want to try my favoured trick of a punch in the ribs. My pals certainly wouldn't pull any punches so I might finish up in hospital with a stoved-in rib cage and all my internal organs shunted over to one side.

Think, Bill. Think. I had to have something wrong with me that prevented running. That way you kill two birds with one stone. If you can't run, you can't charge down the beach into the freezing surf.

How about a broken toe? I could stub my foot on a wall. No, too painful and anyway, there aren't too many walls that leap in front of you while you're in threes and part of a mass crowd of five hundred soldiers.

How about a broken arm? Whoa! Too radical. Anyway, you can still run 'cos there's nothing wrong with your legs. I've seen blokes running in a sling, with pots on their arm and even with their arm strapped tightly to their body.

So bring it down a measure and consider a broken finger? I could trip over and fall on my hand. No, still too painful and anyway, I might break more than one finger and I need all my fingers to play my trombone. And it still wouldn't prevent any running. Think again.

Perhaps something wrong with my eye? No good. Other than becoming permanently blind, your eyes are not connected to your legs so you could still run even with only one eye. I've seen it.

THINK!

What about piles… haemorrhoids… 'bunches of grapes'? I've had these before, just after P Coy. Probably brought on by the strains of P Coy. That would work. Piles definitely stop you running. In fact, running aggravates piles and encourages the appearance of more grapes while you're running. That's it. piles are the answer.

On the morning of a run, I went to the toilet. Sitting there I took a deep breath and pushed with all my might. I held this stance for as long as I could hold my breath. Nothing. OK, try again. Again, nothing although I was beginning to feel a little uncomfortable down there. My sphincter was beginning to complain. I think one more push should do it. It did. Down dropped the grapes.

On my way to the M.Os office I met Drummy.

"Where are you going? Why aren't you dressed for a run?"

"I'm going sick, sir."

"What? You're skiving!"

"No, sir. I've genuinely got something wrong."

"What?"

A little louder, "I said I've genuinely got something wrong." I heard him the first time but let's have a private laugh.

"I heard what you said. I meant what's wrong with you?"

"Oh. Sorry, sir. I thought you said 'what' 'cos you misheard what I said."

"What? No, WHAT... IS... WRONG... WITH... YOU?"

"Sir. I mean no disrespect, but you don't have to speak to me in that tone... Like an imbecile. I heard you the first time."

"Why are you going sick?"

"I've got something wrong sir."

"If I have to ask you again, I'll put you in jail. What's wrong with you?"

I could see his patience was beginning to wear a bit thin so I decided to bring a holt to this inane, but satisfying for me, discussion.

"It's private."

"You're in the army, son. There's nothing private about you except your rank."

I take a deep breath and blow this out like I was exasperated.

"I've got piles, sir."

"What?"

A bit louder, "I'VE GOT PILES, SIR."

He took a deep breath and let it out slowly, "Piles of what?"

"Piles of haemorrhoids, sir," looking embarrassed even though I wasn't.

"Haemorrhoids? You're skiving."

"No, sir. Do you want to take a look?"

"NO! I DON'T WANT—"

I interrupted his snarl. "Better still, sir, come with me then both you and the M.O. can look at the same time."

With that comment he caved in.

"Get off with you. And I want to see your medical chit when we return from the run. And I'll be talking to the M.O. sometime today".

"Yes sir."

I knew that even if Drummy did go see the M.O. he wouldn't get any information because doctors have a code of silence when it comes to discussing their patients' ails.

Sat outside the M.Os office I kept up the pushing to encourage my piles to stay right where they were. When I heard the welcoming, "Next!" I entered the surgery and declined a seat in front of the desk. The doc bent me over, parted the cheeks of my arse and laughed, "Oh wow! Best ones I've seen since med school!" I must have done a good job...

"I'd better put you on light duties for a while." What an obliging M.O.

"Sir. Can I please have an extra light duties chit to give to the Drum Major?"

"What's it got to do with him?"

"He doesn't believe I've got anything wrong".

"He doesn't, does he?? I'll have a word with him when he returns from the run! If you see him first send him to me."

I never had the pleasure of seeing Drummy, that day, to let him know that the M.O. wanted a word. But Drummy kept off my back for the rest of the tour...

CHAPTER 20
Bill's Party Time

During our time in Bermuda the band did a gig at the Southampton Princess Hotel. A posh place, at the time. It might still be posh. I don't know. Who knows? I've not been back to Bermuda since that tour.

As payment for the gig, the band was allowed free access to the hotel's disco, located in its basement. We all got cleaned up, put on our best civvies (the only civvies we had with us) and we walked up the hill to the venue. Down to the basement and we showed our military I.D. cards for entry. My mate 'M' and I had been designated by the band sergeant-major to keep our boys in line.

The disco room was a long, fairly narrow room, with a three-metre corridor from the entrance. On entry we saw all the low-level tables, surrounded by chairs, in rows down each side of the room with the disco gear up against the rear wall. Down there was also a smallish dance floor in front of two huge speakers far too large for the size of the room and guaranteed to make the dancers and anyone sitting at the nearest tables deaf for about a fortnight!

You entered the room via a short corridor, this forming a reversed and inverted L-shape to the left-hand side of the room. Up against the wall around the corner of this L-shape was a table and two chairs which my mate and I picked for our stay. Far enough away from the speakers that our deafness would last only three days, hidden from the entrance door, back to the wall so we could watch the whole room, and nice and dark. An ideal place to keep watch on the rest of our mates. We could also see the entrance, behind us.

In front of us the tables and chairs soon filled with an assortment of 1 Para guys, women from around town and blokes that all thought they were the best thing since sliced bread. The blokes didn't like the 1 Para contingent 'cos they had got in for free and they were chatting up all the spare women that had arrived unaccompanied. They were better looking than the local blokes, anyway. And we had also got there thirty minutes before everyone else and had taken all the best tables where they could chat up the women without having to shout. The local blokes had to contend with the tables nearest the disco speakers.

We arrived early because we'd heard that a delegation of matelots was due to visit the disco, having been given a night off from a U.S. Navy ship, anchored nearby. We couldn't have them getting the pick of the best women!

The night went well. The chatting up was successful and our boys commandeered the dance floor for much of the time. 'M' and I were slowly getting drunk and there weren't too many skirmishes. Any brandishing of handbags by the men was immediately put down by the bouncers disguised as waiters. Although no one was fooled by this disguise because the bouncers had crew cuts, broken noses, necks as thick as tree trunks, biceps like the legs of a grand piano and hands the size of shovels. And the waiters never seemed to be conveying drinks anyway. The agitators were quickly ejected and 'M' and I never needed to get involved.

As the night progressed into early morning 'M' and I were beginning to get bored with listening to repeats of the records. We had been drinking beer from bottles about the size of Coca-Cola bottles and had a good collection of these on the table in front of us. 'M' slipped one of these empty bottles onto the end of his little finger and was casually swinging this between his knees as we discussed the merits of staying, or going to bed.

About eight semi-drunk, noisy matelots in unform had just entered the room and had congregated in the entrance corridor, scrutinising the area for any spare women and giving our guys the evil eye. They didn't go un-noticed by the waiters.

'M' and I decided to go to bed and we were just about to stand up when all hell was let loose.

It was an accident. It was most surreal! 'M' couldn't have known what would happen! It just could not have been predicted... Could it?

The whole room went into a sort of slow-motion mode, exaggerated by the flashing strobe lights, as the bottle flew off 'M's finger. We watched it gracefully float through the air, slowly somersaulting over people's heads, and we just stared as it coasted down onto the table immediately in front of ours. In real time the bottle crashed into the collection of bottles and glasses on that table, scattering them, smashing them and spraying drink everywhere.

The crash was even louder than the music and everything went quiet as the DJ turned the music off to see what the commotion was. Everyone in the room turned round to see why women had cried out in surprise and look to the waiters for some action.

In that single solitary moment, just as everyone turned to look in our direction, 'M' and I stood up in unison and quickly turned to look back at the collection of noisy matelots, congregated around the entrance. We didn't speak to each other, we just stood up and turned round.

The look on the matelots faces was sheer horror as they saw the waiters bulldozing through the crowds towards them. Tables flew, chairs flew, drinks flew, people flew and 'M' and I just sat down to watch the mayhem. With opened mouths the matelots all held up their hands in submission as the waiters ploughed into them and there ensued a noisy tussle in the entrance corridor as the waiters shifted up a gear to eject the "trouble makers". Matelots hats flew, shoes flew, fists flew, shirts got ripped and noses got flattened.

'M' and I sat there looking at each other, stifling our belly laughs as our shoulders bounced up and down.

The matelots got the blame for throwing bottles, the poor saps, but 'M' and I knew they had done nothing wrong! More importantly we both knew that we, or the rest of our mates in 1 Para, wouldn't be ceremoniously ejected by the waiters so we helped tidy up the room and carried on with our party at the disco until sunrise.

The matelots? I guess that they would have had some explaining to do when they returned to their ship with black eyes, bandaged heads, torn clothes, missing hats (and shoes) and cursing their own rogue genes for a night to forget!

Chapter 21
Bill's DTL

 May 1973. We had had just two months at home after leaving Bermuda but it was time to pack up and do some more flying. My regiment was posted to Polemidhia Camp, in the Greek sector of Cyprus, for a nine-month unaccompanied posting.

We swapped our world-famous red berets for blue ones and became part of UNFICYP, The United Nation's Forces in Cyprus.

I was also promoted to L/Cpl during my stay in Cyprus. Surprisingly, my rogue gene had not hindered this but unsurprisingly it had its sights set on another possibility.

Although the weather was great and we had lots of time at the beach, facilities on the camp were a bit basic.

We were told that the camp was originally built by Major-General Charles George Gordon CB (1833 – 1885), also known as Gordon of Khartoum. Despite the alleged age of the camp the huts were in a remarkably good condition. No leaks when it rained, the windows all opened and closed easily and, surprisingly, no wood rot.

The camp was built on a hill, accessed via a road running up the hill from Limassol, a coastal town. It was a large collection of huts housing a battalion (five hundred men) of soldiers, a canteen and outdoor cinema, a company office, officer's quarters, mess hall (that's a dining room, to you non-military persons), a medical hut, a company stores hut, a guard hut, a drill square (drill = practise marching), a shower hut, a band practice hut, a chapel and, importantly, a DTL. Each of the huts for soldiers' quarters accommodated six men.

DTL?

I've been back to Cyprus a couple of times since I left the army and I found that the camp no longer exists, except for a couple of huts, and the town has changed out of all recognition. Even the DTL has disappeared.

DTL??

Okay, okay, no need to shout. I heard you ask, "What's a DTL?" the first time.

DTL is an abbreviation for Deep Trench Latrine. In short, it's a bog (that's a toilet, to you non-military persons).

A deep trench is cut into the ground. This is really, really deep, maybe six metres deep, so you don't want to fall in it or you'll hurt whatever part of your body you land on. You don't want to fall in it anyway in view of what it's used for! The trench is as long as you want it, the camp's DTL was long enough to house four cubicles.

Okay, you build, in timber, a floor and a long rectangular open topped box to cover the trench. Upside down this box is tall enough for you to sit on, and holes slightly smaller than your toilet pan at home have been cut into the bit you sit on. You then permanently fix a toilet seat over each hole. There are two reasons for fixing a toilet seat over the hole; first, aesthetically it looks like a toilet and second, it's more comfortable than sitting on a sharp-edged sawn hole. Finally, each seat is then walled in to provide a bit of privacy and a hut, similar to those that we slept in, is constructed over the top.

Having said that there are no doors on the cubicles so privacy is at a minimum. Stand a roll of bog paper next to each seat and voila! A DTL. No need to knock when you go in because there were no women in our regiment (at the time) and when you get in you can easily see if there are any cubicles that are free to use. Our DTL was used by officers and other ranks alike.

There are no water cisterns to flush. You just dump what you want to dump straight down the hole into the trench. The microbes then take over and break down the solids into mush, assisted by huge volumes of urine, which dissipates into the surrounding soil. Being exposed to the elements (i.e. no doors, window frames with no windows and copious ventilation holes in the walls) there is very little smell. Efficient, eh? Now you know what a DTL is.

As previously mentioned, all ranks shared our DTL. We were even given permission not to salute if we shared the DTL with an officer, although officers had to be given preference and moved to the front of any queue.

Frequently I waited, patiently squeezing my buttocks together, only to get to the front of the queue inwardly telling my weary buttocks, "Hang on a bit... Won't be long now," and an officer nonchalantly walks in front of me and takes my place in the next available cubicle. Rogue genes really test one's resolve...

One day a couple of my mates decided to get back at the

regiment's RSM. Another abbreviation, for Regimental Sergeant-Major. Now this guy is responsible for security, discipline, organisation and anything else the officers don't want to do. He is evil! Although he is a non-commissioned officer he has the power to chastise commissioned officers. Commissioned officers — second lieutenants and upwards — are the ones who have been to Sandhurst Military Academy and they wear 'pips' on their shoulders to let everyone know that they have been to Sandhurst Military Academy. The RSM is one step down from being a commissioned officer but he is not, by far, as polite as a commissioned officer.

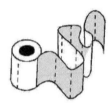 One thing to bear in mind, about DTL's, is that there is, inevitably, a large volume of methane gas in the vicinity of DTL's. Methane is a gas created by the stuff you dump down the hole into the trench, along with other noxious gases, and it's flammable! The presence of methane is a good reason why they built DTL's at least one hundred metres away from all the other huts.

So my mates decided to take advantage of this chemically created marvel by carrying out an experiment. They threaded a long strip of bog paper through one of the ventilation holes in the back of the bog seat and down into the trench. They then unrolled the remainder of the bog roll out to about thirty metres and laid in wait behind some bushes until the RSM came to the DTL for a 'dump'. They knew precisely when he would come because you could set your watch to absolutely everything he did, that's why he's the RSM... And he was as regular as clockwork.

Giving the RSM a short period to get sat down, my mates

concluded their experiment by lighting their fuse of bog paper and watched, in anticipation of something happening, as the flame meandered towards the DTL. It reached the ventilation hole and disappeared into the DTL.

Then, after a slight pause, there was this 'WHUMPH' as the methane in the trench reacted with the flame.

Now I was innocently making my way to the DTL when this 'WHUMPH' shook the DTL and created a mini earthquake. I stopped dead, not knowing what had happened. As I was looking round in surprise I saw my mates behind the bush, both stifling belly laughs with their hands over their mouths, and the RSM appears from the door of the DTL, holding his trousers and underpants over his arm and cursing anyone and everyone he could observe. He was really turning the air blue, Actually the air was already a sort of murky brown colour, but I didn't fully understand why.

He sees me and shouts, "OI! YOU. COME 'ERE!" I knew he was angry because RSM's don't normally walk around with their trousers and underpants hanging over their arm. They might if they've had a good night in the mess, but this was midday, just after lunch. I ran over to him and stood stiffly to attention.

"WHO DID THIS?" he shouts at me so loudly that I didn't hear much for hours afterwards.

"Don't know, Sir."

"YOU DON'T KNOW? WELL, YOU BLOODY WELL SHOULD!"

"Yes, sir... No sir, I was just coming for a dump and I heard this 'WHUMPH' and you appeared out of the DTL."

"WELL, YOU CAN GET TWO MEN AND CLEAN UP THAT MESS IN THE DTL."

"Yes, sir. Why me, sir? I've not done anything?"

"I SAW YOU FIRST. NOW GET ON WITH IT!"

With that, he storms off. I watched him shout and swear his way towards the shower hut. The whole of his arse was covered in shit. At the concealment bush he stops when he sees my mates crouching down.

"WHAT ARE YOU TWO DOING?"

"We've been ordered to do some gardening by Corporal Pollard, sir."

The RSM didn't ask why I'd ordered this gardening club.

"WELL, GET OVER TO THE DTL AND HELP HIM CLEAN IT UP!"

"Yes, sir."

With that they ran over to me, still laughing at the success of their experiment.

*

There was a period, during my stay in Cyprus, that I got a bad case of constipation. It's difficult to determine precisely why I got constipated because we were subjected to a regular dose of exercise which, normally, would have obviated the need to go see the camp Doc' to cure my constipation. It must have been something I ate.

Anyway, the doctor's hut was situated some way away from the DTL. A good thirty second walk. After a short wait I was called into the doc's room and I told him about my predicament.

"Hello, Doc. I've got this severe case of constipation. I've not had a dump for well in excess of a week and it's beginning to weigh me down a bit. Honest, it's up to here," I say, holding my hand horizontally across my top lip.

"I've got just the thing for that," Doc says, reaching into a cupboard and handing me a large ball-shaped pill.

Although I have some reservation about whether I can actually swallow this miniature football I pop it into my mouth and take a big gulp to help it on its way down. The doc turns round to face me having squashed his hand into a rubber glove and asks me for the pill.

"I've just swallowed it."

"WHAT?" You're not supposed to swallow it, I was going to insert it into your rectum!"

I looked at him sort of spaced out, like I'd just snorted some white powder.

"Not to worry," he says and shrugs his shoulders. "I don't think it will do you any harm. Anyway, I've got another but before I insert it into your rectum you must understand something crucially important. You've only got twenty seconds to get down the corridor, out the door, across the yard and into the DTL before you have a detonation. Do you think you can make it?"

I look out of the window in the direction of the DTL and after a quick calculation say "No problem."

The doc looks at me and says, "Well I don't want to chance anything so I think we should have a rehearsal. Remember, you've only got twenty seconds to get down that corridor, out the door, across the yard and into the DTL."

"Okay," I say.

The doc shouts, "GO!"

So I jog down the corridor, out the door, across the yard and into the DTL.

I return to the surgery and doc says "No, no, no. You're

supposed to run. You've only got twenty seconds. Try it again and this time get a shift on yourself. GO!"

Down the corridor, out the door, across the yard and into the DTL. Back to the surgery.

"Look, Corporal Pollard. You've only got twenty seconds! You made it in twenty-two seconds, but you would have been too late. If you really get a move on you might make it. Do you understand?"

"Yes sir."

"Okay. Go!"

Down the corridor, out the door, across the yard and into the DTL, this time much faster. Back to the surgery.

"Wow! nineteen seconds. That's good. Shall we go for it properly?"

"Yes please… Sir," forgetting the presence of my rogue gene.

"Okay, I'll take your word for it that you can rocket down there. If you take your trousers off and really pick your feet up you'll get there in time to get sat down and ready for lift-off. Lay on your side with your knees up to your chest."

I did this and he pushes this cannon ball up my arse with his index finger. Withdrawing his hand he shouts, "GO… GO, GO, GO!"

I dash DOWN THE CORRIDOR OUT THE DOOR ACROSS THE YARD AND INTO THE DTL… And re-appear covered in it from head to foot. Shit. In my shirt pocket, up my nose, all across my back and behind my ears.

The doc puts his head out of the window and hangs my trousers on the window catch for me to collect. "You did it! Eighteen seconds! What went wrong?"

"The DTL was full of officers, sir…"

CHAPTER 22
Bill's Mozzie Net

 Prior to leaving the UK we had all been issued with a copious supply of Paludrine anti-malarial tablets. On arrival at Polemidhia Camp we were all issued with a mosquito net. A "Mozzie" net. There was a good reason for this. During the summer months the island is plagued by mosquitos.

On top of this, the camp was also rife with spiders. Now, you either love spiders or you hate spiders. Personally, I prefer to just leave them alone. They do, after all, perform an important task of keeping the flies and vermin down. But there are times that humans and spiders just don't mix well.

Sleeping under a mozzie net is a little claustrophobic at first but once you've got used to the claustrophobia you hardly notice the net's there. However, one of the squaddies just could not cope with his claustrophobic mozzie net and he left it hanging behind his bed head at night.

There are several types of nasty spiders throughout Cyprus:

The Cyprus Widow, or Black Widow Spider.

The European Tarantula.

The Wolf Spider, also called the "Cyprus Tarantula".

The Jumping Spider.

The Mediterranean Recluse Spider.

These are just a few found in Cyprus, and I've seen them all. Google them to see what they look like and what they can do to you.

Now these spiders don't give you much of a bite. Mostly, their bites are no more painful than a bee sting. It's what happens when they bite that is important to know. They don't exactly bite. They inject with hollow fangs that pump toxic chemicals into the injection area. Some are really toxic, and life threatening without immediate treatment.

Generally, spiders will run away at the first signs of danger to them, and they will only use their fangs in defence. Even the common garden spider, here in the UK, can give you a painful bite if you tease it, so it doesn't pay to make life difficult for any spider. The most common cause of spider bites anywhere is rolling onto them when you are in bed. They like nice warm, dark places and often rest in a folded T-shirt, or blanket or loose sock… or under a bedsheet.

OK. Back to the squaddie who didn't like to use his mozzie net.

At reveille this chap could not be roused. His mates shook him but he remained limp and lifeless. The medic was called. After a brief inspection to make sure he was still alive it was decided that he should be taken to the RAF hospital at Akrotiri. On lifting him up the squaddies found a Wolf Spider clinging to his back. "CATCH HIM! CATCH HIM!" shouts the medic and a cup was unceremoniously plopped on top of the spider on the guy's back. It was budged into a jar, the lid screwed on and it was taken to hospital with the guy.

I never heard whether the squaddie survived the bite, but we were all given specific orders to use our mozzie nets from then onwards.

*

From Cyprus the band was flown to Tehran, Iran, to perform a marching display and evening concert for a UK VIP and his guests. We were there for about three days, being shown off to the Iranian authorities and we had a good time.

On return to our camp, I found that some thieving rat squaddie had swapped my mozzie net for a tattered piece of netting that was covered in pieces of black insulation tape where holes had appeared. It was a mess, a disaster, a really poor example of a mozzie net. The swap could only have been done by one of the electricians from the contingent of R.E.M.E. squaddies. I took this rag to the stores to be exchanged.

"What's wrong with that one?" asks the storeman.

"It's rubbish. It won't even keep a puff of fag smoke out, let alone mozzies."

"Can't exchange it."

"Why not?"

"Haven't got any. See if you can scrounge some insulating tape from the R.E.M.E. guys for the holes."

This was not good news and it was more than a

coincidence that the band had been absent for a few days. I cursed my rogue gene for sending me to Tehran and decided to hatch a plan with my mates.

Somehow, I should get on light duties. Then, while the battalion was on a road walk and run, I could swap my net with someone in the R.E.M.E. hut. It was time to bring my piles back into play.

Yep, the doc agreed that a road run wasn't the best thing for piles and he gave me five days light duties while the bunch of grapes poking out of my arse shrunk back into place. On road run day I quickly swapped my rag with a mozzie net that was in extremely good condition, from the R.E.M.E. hut. I'd loved to have seen this poor sap's face when he got back from the run!

There was an enquiry 'cos the net I exchanged belonged to an NCO. Straight away he accused me of theft because he had, "Seen my bed with this rag hanging over it." Pure fiction. All the occupants of my hut always kept our door closed to keep the feral cats out, so how did he know that the rag had come from my bedspace? Unless he was the one who swapped it.

Anyway, the enquiry came to nothing because I had written my name on my new mozzie net with an indelible pen, and to support this the storeman actually confirmed that he saw me write my name on the mozzie net when it had first been issued to me.

The storeman was considered to be a good bloke by all the band and he was never short of free drinks at the canteen.

I suspect, however, that he knew who he had issued the rag to, in the first place...

CHAPTER 23
Bill's Broken Neck

Most of our free time in Cyprus was spent down at the beach. Lots of sun, sand, sea and relaxation.

At the weekends we were transported down to the beach at RAF Akrotiri, on the southern tip of Cyprus, by a big white RAF bus. Here there was a private beach for RAF personnel but we were permitted to use this providing we didn't get too rowdy and disturb the regulars.

The water was warm, but you had to wade out quite a distance to have a decent swim because it was shallow, just covering one's knee caps.

If we fancied a swim during the week, we got a taxi down to a hotel in Limassol. The manager there was extremely obliging and didn't charge us anything to use his beach or pool. I think that was because he had relatives working in the canteens on camp. An alternative was a taxi to Lady's Mile beach, a more public place but with more facilities.

There were lots of places one could explore but transport was essential. Most of the time we cadged a lift from one of our Land Rovers, on a run to take the sick, dead or dying to hospital or pick something up from the RAF base. Paphos or Larnaca were nearest and these places were tourist hot-spots. The single guys could chat up some women while we were there and the tourists usually paid for all the drinks, so we were guaranteed a good time.

Most evenings we dossed around camp and watched whatever film was being shown on the large open-air screen (a tall wall) adjacent to one of the canteens. If we fancied a night out our favoured haunt was Warrior Square, in Limassol. This place was the red-light district of Limassol. On the day we arrived in Cyprus the RSM got the whole battalion together on the square and gave us all the run-down. What not to do while we were in Cyprus.

Warrior Square was, apparently, out of bounds so what was the first place we visited? Yep, you've got it. If you became a "regular" at some of the bars you got free drinks on the basis that you would bring your friends to become "regulars". Although I had a favoured bar my mates and I sometimes cruised the bars for free drinks, 'cos we were "regulars" in all of them.

On one of our sorties to the beach my mates and I were challenged to a game of Donkey by some of the local Greek wannabes. They were wannabes because they admired our uniforms, admired our six-packs and they admired the way the Greek girls followed us around. They genuinely wanted to be in our army.

You don't know what Donkey is?

Up to your waist in water, you swim under your pal's legs and then stand up while he sits on your shoulders. He bends his legs backwards, around your midriff, holding tightly onto your lower back. You are the donkey and he is the donkey rider. Okay, there are two teams of opposing Donkeys, with riders, facing each other. On the word, opposing Donkeys move towards each other and the riders have to displace their opposition. By any means possible. Shoving, wrestling, even boxing. We didn't call it "boxing" 'cos the Queensbury rules were non-existent. It was just a punch on the nose when you knew that you couldn't unseat your opponent by any legal means. If anyone complained you apologised, "Oh, sorry. I thought you were boxing!"

Anyway, there we were, donkey fighting this team of Greeks. I was a donkey. When we got into it my rider decided to have a laugh at my expense. Or perhaps it was my rogue gene influencing his rogue gene to inflict a surprise on me. Regardless of who, or what, thought of it, my mate pretended to be knocked off his donkey (me) and toppled sideways into the water, taking my head with him. Now, if you're knocked off your donkey, you're supposed to relax your legs to let your donkey roam free. Not this clown! He hung on to me. Thinking he had been knocked off, and also thinking he would let go, I stood firm, waiting for him to drop into the water. Not so. My head went sideways, my neck went CRUNCH, and my legs gave way beneath me.

I couldn't move. This idiot was still holding my head under the water with his legs. I was breathing in water and started thrashing around in panic. I heard him laughing, then everything went blank. I passed out.

Next thing I knew I was laying on the beach being kissed by a gorgeous Greek woman. Opening my eyes, I realised that it wasn't a kiss in the normal sense, and the gorgeous Greek woman was about two hundred years old! She was giving me mouth-to-mouth resuscitation. Retching up a lung full of water

I sat up to recover my senses. After a few minutes I decided that I'd had enough beach for the day, pulled on my tracksuit bottoms and went to find a lift back to camp. I'll see to the brainless fool later.

That evening, while watching the film, I felt really weird. Dizzy, neck ached, knees wobbly, vision a bit, well, not quite in focus. I decided that I'd possibly got too much sun and went to bed early.

Next morning reveille reminded us all that it was time to get up. I couldn't lift my head off the pillow. Not because I was still tired. I'd had a really peaceful night's sleep. I just couldn't lift my head off the pillow. I asked my mate to help me and he gently lifted my head while I sat upright. Neither could I swivel my head. It seemed to be locked in place. Unmoveable. I tried nodding. Nope, no chance. I decided to go sick.

The doc looked at me. My neck was, by now, as stiff as a plank. I told him what I'd been up to yesterday and he immediately called in his medic to hold my head while he put a neck brace on me. I was dashed to the hospital at RAF Akrotiri under a blue light. After an emergency X-ray I was strapped into traction. I had a broken neck.

I couldn't believe it when the hospital doc told me that he was amazed at how lucky I was to still be able to feel my toes and fingers!

I spent the next five days in traction, my neck gradually being stretched back into place. During those five days the RAF nurses thought it hilarious to tease me with displays of exposed nipples, bare breasts just out of my reach, and accidental "strokes" of my balls while they changed my sheets, knowing I could do nothing about it.

Frivolities came to an end when, after several inspections

and X-rays, the doc declared that my neck was healing nicely and he decided to set me free from my restraints. The nurses all suddenly kept at least an arm's length away from me for some reason…

I was released from hospital and returned to my unit wearing a neck brace. I had this on right until the time came to pack our suitcases for the journey home. I wore it on every parade, tattoo, concert and display. Bloody uncomfortable. Especially in the Cyprus heat and even more so when I was playing my trombone.

The neck brace was, however, a good pull for free drinks in Warrior Square!

CHAPTER 24
Bill's Late Dump

The battalion had just spent several months in Cyprus, unaccompanied. When we returned to Aldershot on the twenty-fifth of October, 1973, there was talk of a population explosion from the 1 Para wives in nine months' time! I couldn't begin to explain who started this rumour, or why...

It is twentieth of January, 1974. We had been given just three months to reintroduce ourselves to our wives and children again before we were packing up for another tour. This time to Nanyuki, sat on the Equator in Kenya.

Once more, the RAF would accommodate us on their jet planes and once more the RAF hostesses "practised" their customer service skills on a couple of the blokes. Lucky fellas!

Our flight was a long one and we had to call in to a refuelling station on the island of Bahrain, in the Persian Gulf. I guess that the island has changed a lot since then, but back in those days the place where we landed was pure desert. Just sand for as far as you could see.

The plane parked up next to a couple of small sheds; one with the refuelling equipment and the other a single toilet buzzing with flies. That's all there was. Just a couple of small sheds and lots of sand.

We disembarked while the plane was refuelled. The only thing we could do was either have a game of football or sit in the shade of the plane's wings. The heat was blistering. Although we had become acclimatised to the Cyprus heat our acclimatisation had worn off during our brief stay back home.

It took a couple of hours to refuel the plane, although the time just floated by. I sat there, in the shade of the toilet hut, and when the queue had died down, I decided to stretch my legs and go for a dump. Nobody else wanted to use the toilet so I thought it was the ideal time. No rush. Nobody opening the door asking how long I was going to be. Nice and casual. Plenty of time to cogitate. Plenty of time to get a bit of shuteye in this shady bit of desert.

Sat there, half asleep, I felt my feet vibrate. No, it wasn't my feet. It was the ground. And what's that rumbling? I shook myself awake. Startled I heard the noise made by a plane's engines... Our plane's engines! Rapidly wiping my arse and pulling up my trousers I dashed out of the toilet to hear the engines roar and see the plane dashing down the dirt runway. I also saw one of my mates, waving goodbye to me through a window. I'm sure he was laughing. I know my rogue gene was.

Two words came to mind; shit and bollocks!

It was no good waving to attract the pilot's attention. I knew he would not waste fuel by turning round to pick me up. As I watched the plane disappear into the clouds I looked around. Nothing but sand and two huts. At least I could have a piss whenever I wanted...

Then it occurred to me that perhaps there was a telephone in the refuelling hut. How else would the pilots communicate with the main refuelling base somewhere else on this desolate wasteland?

Slowly walking over to the hut, at the same time calling my rogue gene all the unprintable names I could think of, I wondered what punishment awaited me when... If I ever re-joined my unit? I would surely get busted back down to the rank of Private (I had been promoted to L/Cpl in Cyprus).

Yes, there was a phone in the hut! A field phone. I picked this up and wound the handle to charge the phone. Putting it to my ear I heard, "Central. How much fuel do you require?"

"Hello?"

Again, "Central. How much fuel do you require?"

"Oh. No. No fuel. I need some help."

"Help with what, sir. Instructions are on the wall in front of you."

"No, I don't need instructions, I need some help."

"To refuel, sir?"

"No. I've missed my plane."

"Has the plane refuelled, sir?"

"Yes, and stop calling me sir."

"Sorry sir. How can I help you?"

"I've missed my plane."

"I'll put you through to the nearest refuelling helpline."

"No! I don't need to refuel. I need some help," desperation creeping in.

"If you don't need any fuel, why are you calling Central?"

"I'VE MISSED MY PLANE! I NEED TO GET OFF THIS ISLAND!"

"Please don't shout sir. Your signal is being received loud and clear."

"Look... What's your name?"

"This is Central sir. Which plane are you booked on?".

"I know it's Central, and stop calling me sir. I was on the flight from RAF Abingdon, in the UK, to Mombasa, Kenya."

"Do you know the flight number sir?"

"No."

"Okay, I'll put you through to Transportation."

"NO, WAIT. I NEED—"

The phone buzzed and clicked as she cut me off. Silence. I drew a deep breath and blew this out through my cheeks. I was just about to put the phone down when it rang. I heard, "Transport. How can I help?"

"I need instructions on how to get off Bahrain. I've missed my plane."

"There is no UK military airport in Bahrain, sir. Where do you want to get to?"

"Mombasa."

"From where, sir?"

"Don't call me sir. I'm trying to find a flight out of Bahrain."

"We don't fly to Bahrain airport, sir. How did you get there?"

"No, I'm not at the airport. I'm at an RAF refuelling station."

"Oh. okay, sir. I'll put you through to Central. Please ask for Refuelling."

"NO! WAIT! I DON'T NEED FUEL, I NEED HELP! TO GET TO MY UNIT IN KENYA!"

"Oh. Sorry sir. I'll put you through to Customer Services."

"NO! WAIT! Please let me explain what I want, and why I want it."

"Okay, sir. Fire away."

I gave the guy my name, rank and number and explained my predicament. There was a silence that I thought was ominous, but the guy came back to me. "I think you should talk to my Station Commander, sir. I'll get a message to him. Please stand by to receive his call."

"Will do," I replied.

It didn't take long for the Station Commander to come back to me.

"Is that you, Corporal Pollard?"

"Yes, sir."

"Okay. I understand that you are at the refuelling station on Bahrain. Just explain how you came to be stranded there."

I went through my story one more time.

"Okay. I understand. Do you want me to inform your unit?"

"No, please don't do that, sir. I'm sure they'll find out soon enough."

"Okay. Message received. Now look, there's a U.S. Airforce plane calling in to your location in about three hours. Can you manage 'till then?"

"No problem, sir. I've got a toilet, so what more do I need?"

"Good man. I'll contact the U.S. Airbase at Cyprus to get them to expect you."

"Thank you, sir," with a sigh of relief.

I settled down behind the refuelling shed to await my ride.

The Americans really know how to entertain. They had a bar full of booze and a stereo blaring American songs all the way to Mombasa. And their hostesses were made up like film stars, every one of them gorgeous. The crew just wouldn't let this "limey" get any rest with their constant questions and banter. When we arrived in Mombasa there was no customs station to go through. The air crew, with me, were just ushered through the back doors. As I'm making my way out of the airport I was wondering how I could get to Nanyuki when I suddenly saw a 1 para Land Rover parked in a loading yard.

I quickly climbed over the tailgate and sat in the back. The driver had come to the airport to pick up some stores for the Nanyuki camp. His look of surprise was a picture when he put the stores in the back of his wagon. "What the f*** are you doing here, Bill?"

"You don't want to know."

I arrived at camp and looked for someone who might know what was happening. I met the Bandmaster.

"Where have you been, Cpl Pollard?"

I thought I'd better come clean about my adventure on Bahrain and began, "I went for a dump..." But was interrupted."

"Okay, okay. Did you go to the briefing? Do you know what's happening?"

"I was hoping you would tell me, sir."

So what just happened? No bollocking. No shouting. No reprimand. I bet he never even missed me. He thinks I've just been for a dump down at the Camp's DTL!

"Draw out a tent and pitch it with the rest of the band down there."

CHAPTER 25
Bill's Tent

Down in the jungle, living in a tent. Better than a prefab... No rent.

The "temporary" camp at Nanyuki was located in the middle of nowhere. I had to erect my own tent when I found the band's pitch. That was the last thing I needed after a long flight and my annoyed mutterings were about why the advance party had not already done this. What had they been doing for the past three weeks that they had spent on "advanced logistics"?

We later found out that there was a small village about fifteen minutes from the camp, Simba's Village. We wondered if that was a good enough magnet to divert the advance party from setting up the camp. Having made a quick recce we decided that it was, in view of the many "attractions" this village of numerous huts and half naked women had.

Anyway, these tents were one-man bivvies. Not the modern circular type you can get for a fishing trip that one sees nowadays, but a pitched canvas thing that required two tent poles and guy ropes at each end. I collected my tent from the "temporary" tented stores — one of five hundred tents that had been stored in a central forces store, in the UK and taken to Kenya specifically for this posting — and I unrolled my temporary home for the next month or two.

Spoiler alert! Rogue gene stalking me!

Guess what? I found that I had only one tent pole.

It's blatantly obvious that my rogue gene had struck again, so I went back to the stores and asked the storeman for a tent pole.

He looked at me a bit spaced out and asked, "Don't you want a tent to go with that?"

"No, I've got a tent but there's a pole missing."

"What have you done with it?"

"Nothing, the pole was missing when I drew out the tent."

"Not the tent, the tent pole?"

"I've just said. It wasn't inside the tent."

"So you've got a tent, but no tent pole?"

"That's correct... No, I've already got one tent pole."

"So why do you want another tent. Isn't that a bit selfish?"

"I don't want another tent. I just need another tent pole."

"But you've just told me you've got one?"

"But I need two and I'VE ONLY GOT ONE... Tent poles that is. MY TENT NEEDS TWO TENT POLES AND I'VE ONLY GOT ONE."

There was a pregnant pause and the storeman's face lit up in recognition of the misunderstanding that had just taken place.

"Ah! I know what's happened. You've got a type one bivvy and you should have a type two."

"Type two? What's that?"

"It's a tent."

"What's the difference between a type one tent and a type two tent?"

"Well, a type one tent is a pitched canvas type with two tent poles and guy ropes at each end, and a type two tent is a round canvas type with smaller guy ropes all around its perimeter, and it requires just one tent pole. You shouldn't have a type one tent".

"OK, then can I have a type two tent, please?"

"But you've already got a tent."

"You've just told me I should have a type two tent."

"Correct."

"Well can I have one?"

"Sorry, none left. That's why I issued type ones."

"Well can you please give me a second tent pole for my type 1 tent?"

"Can't."

"Why not?"

"Type one tents are all gone. You were a bit slow getting here and all the band's senior NCO's have bagged the type ones for their kit. You'll have to go ask the Bandmaster if he'll turf his kit out and let you have his type one."

There was as much chance of the BM co-operating with that request as I had of becoming a captain within the next ten minutes.

I suddenly had this bright flash of an idea. Forget this insane conversation and go and pinch someone else's tent pole.

While returning to my pitch I scanned the area for someone who was also a bit slow in pitching their tent, and someone who also had a type one tent. I homed in on this potential idiot and approached him from the direction of the stores.

He had just unrolled his tent and all its components (two tent poles, two guy ropes and eight tent pegs) were somewhat scattered around his pitch. I offered to help and picked up a corner of his tent. I said to him, "Have you checked all the components? These types of tents sometimes have a tent pole missing."

He replied, "No, not yet. Let's have a look," and we proceeded to check his components.

Initially, he looked pleased that everything was present and correct until I told him that, "This tent pole is mine," picking up one of his. "I've just drawn it out of the stores 'cos my tent was issued with only one tent pole. That's how I know that some of these type 1 tents are missing a tent pole."

"Bollocks!" he said. "I'm gonna have to go all the way back to the stores to get another tent pole."

"Looks that way," says I, and the poor sap marches off to request another tent pole from the stores.

Anyway, I finished pitching my own tent and then, looking at my watch, decided it was tea time, so I head off towards the "temporary" tent cook house. Passing the stores on the way I overheard this strange conversation…

"I've just said. It wasn't inside the tent."

"So, you've got a tent, but no tent pole."

"That's correct… No, I've already got a tent pole".

"So why do you want another tent?"

I wondered if his rogue gene was related to mine in some way and I got this definite feeling of deja vu, in more ways than one…

CHAPTER 26
Bill's Insect Invasions

When I was knee high to a gnat, Dad brought home a tent that had been given to him by some bloke he did a favour for. My brothers and I would disappear for days during the school holidays, camping at a place called Ford Brook, just off Ford Lane, near Eckington. Great fun. We caught our own meals; Trout from the brook with tins of beans, peas and potatoes appropriated from Mum's pantry.

I'm grown up now and living in a tent in Kenya. Now, living in a tent isn't much fun when you have to squash all your belongings into it and maintain a pristine appearance.

The art, we learned, was to hang up our whites — the white jacket that we wore on parades, concerts, etc. — on a looped rope attached to the tent pole at the head end of your tent, and neatly fold the rest of your kit and store this in your suitcase. What we also learned, very quickly, was that anything (and I mean anything) that you put directly on the floor was eaten by termites. It didn't matter what. Sleeping bags, suitcases, the clothes in your suitcase, socks when you go to bed, clothes you leave lying around. The termites even had a good go at your boots. And it didn't take them long to demolish your kit. A few hours and it's pulp.

So, after a few full kits had been reduced to dust the order was announced from above that, "We do not, under any circumstances, keep anything other than the legs of our camp beds directly on the floor of our tent." They didn't tell us how to suspend our kit in mid-air, so we had to do some lateral thinking.

The senior NCOs came up with a terrific idea. The question they asked themselves was, "Why didn't the fence around the camp get eaten by termites?" Senior NCOs always thought of the good questions. That's why they're senior NCOs. Anyway, the answer, they found out, was that termites didn't like the type of wood that the fence was made of. So... Why not use the fence to construct a platform for your kit?

Excellent question, and the senior NCOs gave instructions to their platoons to remove this fence under cover of darkness and divvy the pieces up to the blokes. Two pieces of fencing each, when laid on the ground, would give support for your suitcase and raise this off the earth. Boots and clothes on top and your kit would be unavailable to the termites. The simplest answer is always the best.

As usual, the band were last in the queue for the pieces of "platform", so we got none because the fence ran out all too soon. After all, one fence just wasn't enough to go round five hundred blokes. The band had to do even more lateral thinking.

When the squaddies disappeared on manoeuvres we sneaked into their tents and nicked their bit of fence. Our senior NCOs raided the squaddie's senior NCOs' tents. Who was to know? As far as anybody was concerned, we had been divvied up, the same as everybody else.

That was the story we stuck to when, hours later, the squaddies returned from their jungle exercise to find their kit reduced to mush. The camp resonated with anguished cursing and swearing, and vociferous threats of, "Whoever nicked my f****** platform is going to f****** die!"

The squaddies were not too pleased…

*

At this point, it's perhaps appropriate to give you a bit of a history lesson on the development of the military band. If you're not interested just skip over this bit, but it's not too long and boring.

Way back in the days of the Red Coats, the soldiers had to march everywhere 'cos they hadn't discovered petrol, yet. Marching is really boring, even today, with nothing to concentrate on except left, right, left, right, left, right, left, right for hours, so someone thought of adding a drum and a drummer. This poor sap had to beat his drum continually to ease the boredom of the marching squaddies. Hard work until someone added more drummers, and then more drummers, until a whole platoon of drummers was formed. They had the job of augmenting the bugle calls so that all the regiment could hear the instructions given by the commanders. A good example of this is the modern day "Beating the Retreat", a military tattoo depicting the troop's call to retreat back into the fort.

Okay, drums are fine, up to a point, but their repertoire is a bit limited, so someone decided to add a flute — a piccolo in today's terms — to play a few tunes while the soldiers marched. Suddenly the troops had flutes and drums. Then a whole load of wind instruments got added. Clarinets, sacbuts, trumpets, horns. Eventually this ensemble evolved into today's military band.

Interesting or what?

Now what many people don't know is that playing an instrument in the forces is supplemental to their prime job of being a soldier, or airman, or matelot. We were always regarded as soldiers first and musicians last. In the two great wars musicians were, in reality, stretcher bearers with guns, as I understood it. When I was in the army this philosophy had been developed to call us medics, primarily assisting the doctors and nurses in the battlefield by providing first aid. Today, of course, the army medical service is a specialised unit requiring years of training.

So, whilst in Kenya 1 Para band was put on medical training to bring them up to the A3 medic level of competency.

We didn't always take our medical training seriously. The staff sergeant providing our training took us out into the scrubland occasionally to put us in the scenario of being "in the field". Most of the time we sat around smoking while we practised bandaging or fitting arm slings. Sometimes the sergeant would throw a curved ball at us to wake us up by shouting questions, with a large degree of urgency, like, "THAT MAN'S CHOKING! HE'S SWALLOWED HIS TONGUE! QUICKLY! WHAT ARE YOU GOING TO DO? HE'S DYING!"

This was answered nonchalantly with, "Blow up his arse," not quite the answer he was looking for, but it created a few laughs.

On one occasion a real medic and I decided to have a walk down to Simba's Village. As we left camp, we saw a pedestrian get knocked over by a van. The medic and I dashed to the scene and shooed all the onlookers away from the guy who was sat on the floor, supporting himself with a hand and looking a bit pale around the gills. Nobody had done anything for the guy, except collect his belongings and unceremoniously dump these into his lap. He was an old guy. He couldn't speak English and we couldn't speak Kenyan but he realised we were trying to help him and he laid back, submissively.

"What you gonna do?" the medic asks.

"Check him for damage."

I immediately checked his body from head to foot to see if there were any breakage. There was. His right leg had been fractured halfway between his kneecap and ankle. I told the medic to provide extension to his leg by holding his foot and gently pulling, to separate the fracture. After a minute or two the medic slowly released the extension so that his leg bones eased back into their correct position. I took the guy's walking stick and splinted his leg with it, using his scarf to tie the splint into place. By now an ambulance had arrived and he was carefully lifted onto a stretcher and into the ambulance for transport to hospital.

The medic related this incident to the staff sergeant on our return to camp. I was immediately promoted to A3 medic… not that that did anything for me.

*

On another occasion I was called to a squaddie's tent to find out why he hadn't woken up at reveille, being the nearest "medic" to him. I was joined by a proper medic and we decided that there wasn't enough room to work properly inside the tent, so we ordered a couple of squaddies to remove the tent.

This done, we could look more closely at the guy comatose on his camp bed. The real medic carefully unzipped his sleeping bag to find the whole of his body covered in great big hairy caterpillars. Huge things covered in hairs.

One of the squaddies tried to pluck one of these monsters from his mate but quickly shot his hand back, as if he had been burnt. We looked at his finger. It had several caterpillar hairs embedded in it.

We decided that the best course of action was to carefully scrape the caterpillars off this guy and drop them on the ground next to his bed. This left him covered with stiff, black hairs. By the time we had finished removing the caterpillars the ambulance had arrived and he was taken to hospital.

We found out, later, that the guy had captured one of these caterpillars and he had kept it in a matchbox. We surmised that the caterpillar "prisoner" must have shouted to its mates for help. I never heard whether the guy recovered or whether he returned to duty.

His rogue gene really did possess a mean streak...

CHAPTER 27
Bill's Rear Party

 We stayed in Kenya for precisely one month. The twentieth of January to the twentieth of February, 1974. It was time to pack up and return home. The band was selected to be the battalion's rear party, packing up the camp and getting the tents and equipment ready for return to central stores back in the UK.

Nothing of value was to be left behind.

I had enjoyed this tour and I will have some good memories of my adventures here, although I would be a little short of kit when we departed.

Why?

It was hot here during the day so we didn't have much use for pullovers, and I had plenty of pairs of socks. We found out that the locals running the stalls down in Simba's village coveted anything woollen.

Although the days were hot, the nights were cold and in the rainy season the locals didn't have very much in the way of dry clothes to change into. So we bundled up what we could and went bartering in the village. Even the senior NCO's.

Sometimes we bartered for cheap trinkets and tourist goods, sometimes the locals gave us a small amount of cash. Sometimes the guys bartered with the half-naked women for tea and something else warm…

It was, of course, illegal to barter one's kit, but who would know? We could always get replacements when we returned to the UK, claiming that the termites had got to the deficiencies before we could protect them. Anyway, the hierarchy in the regiment considered our "acts of charity" to be good for British/Kenyan relationships.

Another "wheeze" with the locals was the confusion over the value of a British ten bob note. It had to be a British ten bob note. Not many of us had one, but those that did exchanged it for the equivalent in cash with our mates. The ten bob notes were then taken to Simba's village to be exchanged for something worth more than ten bob. The locals also coveted our ten bob notes because they thought these were ten-pound notes, and they were over the moon to be told to, "Keep the change."

These transactions took place the day before we departed, just in case the locals caught on…

*

Now, of all the things I enjoyed, the grub was superb considering it had been thrown together in a field kitchen. The cooks excelled themselves with all sorts of different dishes and we always had a full stomach.

In true British army tradition, there

was a guard to keep watch on the camp twenty-four per day during our stay. The guard was selected from the ranks and was managed by the provo sergeant in charge of the "naughty boys". As we didn't have a jail, to house the naughty boys, they were put on twelve hour guard shifts.

The colonel, however, had thought of everything and he ordered that a cauldron was to be acquired and suspended over a fire. A stack of wood was to be permanently piled next to the pot to ensure that the fire under the cauldron never went out. The woodpile and the fire were to be managed by the guard and if the fire went out the offending guards for that night were given an extra guard shift.

The order was given that the cauldron was to be filled with our food scraps and any left-overs from the kitchen. So, we all complied with this order and after every meal we scraped our scraps into the cauldron and the cook supplemented these with the left-overs. Absolutely everything went into the pot. Meat, gravy, potatoes, greens, carrots, biscuits, cake, pudding, custard, tea, coffee, milk… The lot. Absolutely everything and anything edible.

This mix turned into a mushy soup that was kept continuously bubbling by the fire. Every other day the cook would anaesthetise the soup with a tin of curry powder and an urn of cold tea.

This soup was for everyone. It was fantastic! It tasted great, and was available all day and every day. A tasty snack during the day, or an alternative to the main meals, or a hot broth for the guard at night. A brilliant idea. Topped up and was bubbling continuously. Mmmmm!

On the final day of the tour myself and a couple of guys from the rear party were ordered to empty the cauldron and clean this, to be given to No.1. I'll tell you about No.1 in a moment.

The fire was dowsed by some of the pot's content, and the pot was pushed over to empty on the ground. The soup would disperse into the ground and any leftovers would be devoured by the wild animals that frequented the camp while we slept. In the bottom of the pot, we found some unexpected items that couldn't possibly be eaten. Items that were surprising in their presence but, nonetheless, gave the rear party a good laugh.

Several pairs of socks.

A couple of pullovers.

A beret, with cap a badge.

A pair of PT pumps.

Underpants… Many.

An assortment of cutlery which had been accidentally dropped while scraping.

A log from the woodpile.

Empty curry tins.

The starter motor from a Land Rover.

There really is a lot of truth in the old adage, "What the eye doesn't see, the heart can't grieve about."

We buried this lot nice and deep.

*

No.1?

No.1 was a local chap that the RSM had employed to be his right-hand man. No.1 would do anything the RSM asked him to do. He was, in reality, a gofer. Fetch and carry for the RSM, take messages to the colonel, bring messages from the colonel, make the RSM's bed, go to town to buy the RSM's cigarettes, patrol the camp to check the cauldron fire was burning, pick up litter. In fact, anything the RSM wanted him to do. He was proud to be the RSM's No.1 and he carried out his duties diligently. His brother would bring cartons of ice cream to camp, surrounded by ice, and No.1 would patrol the camp shouting, "ICE CREAM. ICE CREAM. I SCREAM, YOU SCREAM, EVERYBODY SCREAM!" It was his way of advertising the fact that the ice cream van was here, and he always sold out.

When the main party, with the RSM, departed from camp No.1 was gutted. He would not, any more, have authority over the small army of local men taken on to maintain the camp. They had all been discharged. Taking pity on him, our company commander enlisted him to assist with the camp clean-up. This perked him up no end.

On the day we were due to leave camp to go to the airport he mooched around, looking for things to do. As the final hours drew to a close, we all knew that he was sadly sat next to his newly acquired cauldron, guarding this and waiting for his brother to pick him up in a battered old truck.

The rear party was putting the finishing touches to the clean-up tasks and was spread around the camp. The company commander then had a job for No.1. He shouted, "No.1?" No response. "No.1?"

Still no response so the whole of the rear party decided to help the company commander locate No.1 by calling, from all corners of the camp, "No.1? No.1? No.1?"

The guy didn't know which way to turn. "No.1?" over here, or, "No.1?" over there, or, "No.1?" behind him. Perhaps it was the, "No.1?" from his left, or the, "No.1?" from his right... He would run a couple of steps, turn and run another couple of steps and turn again to run in a different direction, like a headless chicken.

The company commander was furious. He bellowed, "KEEP QUIET!" and everything went quiet. He then started it all off again by calling, "No.1?" Again, this was followed by dozens of repeated, "No.1?" from everywhere in the camp.

We could tell the company commander wasn't pleased, by his enraged screams of, "QUIET! QUIET! KEEP QUIET!"

There was a short period of silence, about five seconds, then we heard a single, quiet, plaintiff, "No.1?" emanate from somewhere near the sergeant's mess. Everyone's stifled belly laughs were suddenly released into howls of hilarity.

The company commander composed himself and shouted, "Cpl Pollard! Find No.1 for me."
From all corners of the camp came the call, "Cpl Pollard? Cpl Pollard?"

At long last, the time had come for us to get on the trucks and make our way to the airport. No.1 shook every one of our hands as we boarded the trucks and we waved to him as we pulled out of camp.

With thoughts of someday being a bandmaster I was wondering what the future held for me, and my rogue gene, back in Aldershot...

CHAPTER 28
Bill's Impromptu Arrangement

Having returned from Kenya in February, 1974, the band settled down to its summer season of concerts and parades.

It was, by now, a well-known fact that I wanted to go back to Kneller Hall to become a bandmaster (BM). Word just got round and everyone in the band, including the BM, didn't just accept this, they expected me to go. They took it for granted that I was, at some time in the near future, going there.

I was asked to be Music Director for Aldershot's town band, The Aldershot Concert Band. This band was made up of civvy musicians and instrumentalists from the various military bands around Aldershot. They were all top class players. We performed regular concerts in Aldershot Library theatre and my conducting skills significantly improved. My proudest moment with this band was conducting a joint concert with The Hants and Dorset Band TAVR in Aldershot's prestigious theatre, The Prince's Theatre.

I was also invited to become a member of the Royal Aircraft Establishment's (RAE) orchestra in Farnborough. I went in on top trombone. This orchestra was sponsored by the RAE and we performed at several notable venues around Aldershot and London while I was a member, playing a large variety of classical music.

1 Para band rehearsed for a service at St. Martin-In-The-

Fields, the world-famous church in the corner of Trafalgar Square. This was a prestigious gig. It must have been prestigious because the regiment's Director of Music (DoM) was conducting. I can't remember what the gig was for, or what was being celebrated.

The DoM was a captain, and he was responsible for all three regimental bands. He was "the boss" when it came to respect from the bands and bandmasters.

We loaded up a hired coach, the coach driver started his engine and we were just about to set off when someone piped up, "Is that the telephone ringing?" The bandmaster (BM) stopped the coach and asked one of the blokes to answer the telephone in the band room.

He returned a few moments later and says to the BM, "The DoM has asked for you and he wants to speak to Cpl. Pollard."

"What for?" asks the BM.

"Don't know, sir. I didn't ask." You don't ask when an officer gives you an order. You just take it for granted that he knows what he's doing and anyway, if he hasn't mentioned your name, it's got nothing to do with you.

"Did he say why he wanted to speak to Cpl. Pollard?"

"No Sir, didn't ask."

The BM ordered me off the coach and told me to wait outside his office door. He reappeared moments later and told me to speak to the DoM. He then disappeared into the band library. I gingerly picked up the telephone receiver, thinking, "What have I done? Has my rogue gene been up to his tricks again?"

"Cpl. Pollard speaking sir."

"Ah, Cpl. Pollard. Has the bandmaster said anything to you yet?"

"No sir. I didn't ask."

"Well, I've just been notified of a new hymn that wasn't on the original hymn list. The BM tells me that the band doesn't have this in your library so I've just given him the hymn number, but it needs to be arranged from the hymn book. Can you please arrange this in time to arrive at St. Martin-In-The-Fields?"

After a pregnant pause… "I'll try, sir."

"No, don't try. Succeed! This is important."

"Yes sir."

With that we terminated the phone call and I went to the library to meet up with the BM. Between us we gathered a copious supply of blank manuscript cards and the BM thrust the hymn book into my hand. "You'd better get on with it," he says. On the way out of the library I picked up a few pens.

I decided to do a "quick and dirty" arrangement. Stick to the score and don't add any embellishments. Knowing it would probably take about an hour to get to the church I formulated a plan. I firstly went down the aisle of the coach to make sure the guys had enough pens to go round. That done, I started arranging. The flute part came out first. I gave this to one of the flute players with a blank manuscript card and instructed him to copy it for his partner and pass the pen, and a blank card, on to the piccolo player.

Next was the first clarinet part. We had several first, several second and several third clarinet players, so these parts were hastened onto the production line. The first, second and third cornets were then duplicated from the clarinet parts.

Next was the bass line, the euphonium and bass. The euph player could copy the bass part.

Next were the sax parts, first and second alto's and the

tenor saxes. All single player parts so no copying was required. Likewise, with the Eb clarinet and oboe parts.

Finally, the trombones. first, second and third, again single player parts, followed by the first, second and third horns.

I went down the coach aisle to check everything had been transcribed and provide help where it was required. As we pulled into Trafalgar Square, I just managed to put the final touch to the percussion parts.

Phew! Job done.

We were met by the DoM. The first thing he asks of the BM is, "Has that hymn been done?"

The BM replies, "Ask Cpl Pollard."

He approached me, but before he could say anything I popped in with, "All done, sir."

"Well done Cpl Pollard."

The band set up on the balcony. As soon as we were ready the DoM calls me to the front and orders me to, "Tune the band, please, Cpl Pollard." What an honour! Me. A lowly L/Cpl in front of the band with the DoM looking on. There were lots of senior NCO's and, indeed the BM, that could have done this, but the DoM chose me. Having tuned the band, I took the opportunity to try out my arrangement to see if there were any errors. There were none.

The DoM congratulated me and I returned to my seat. Was this a test? A test to see if I was up to being a BM? I don't know, but I like to look back on this incident and think to myself, "Maybe…"

A few weeks later, in July, 1974, I was posted to the Depot, The Parachute Regiment, Browning Bks, to take on my new role as instructor to the young musicians of The Junior

Parachute Company, or JPC. I had come a full circle, back to where I first joined the army. This time I was teaching and I regarded this posting as a great privilege and honour. I was so proud to have been given this position of responsibility.

I was instructed to report to the DoM. I said my goodbyes to my mates in 1 Para and made my way to the Depot.

It struck me that all this happened with absolutely no interference from my rogue gene.

Absolutely none…

CHAPTER 29
Bill's Proud Moments

July, 1974. I was welcomed to the Depot by the DoM, a captain. I liked this guy. He was a quiet spoken chap with a pleasant manner. Friendly. I suppose he must have liked something in me, otherwise why would he have sanctioned my posting to the Depot as an Instructor with JPC? He took me to the band room to introduce me to the band staff and to the young musicians, the boys.

This posting turned out to be the most satisfying job that I had ever done in the army. Best job so far. Best job, that is, until my rogue gene woke up! But I'll return to that thing later. Suffice to say that I couldn't have felt more proud, to have been chosen for this job.

The band room was located on the outskirts of the Depot, adjacent to the playing field. It was a flat roofed, single storey building housing a largish space for band rehearsals, a small library, an instrument store and an office for each of the instructors. It was well kitted out with instruments, music stands and equipment enabling the band to be a self-contained unit.

It was attached to the drum store, a structure mirroring the band room. This was where the young drummers were schooled. So, similarly to the battalion bands, the Depot had its own band and drums platoons.

The band and drums didn't need much staff. For the band there was a Band Sergeant Major (BSM) with the rank of WOII, a full Corporal (Cpl) and a Lance Corporal (L/Cpl), (me). The drums had a Drum Major (D/M) with the rank of WOII and again a Cpl and L/Cpl.

In overall charge of the band and drums was the DoM.

The Depot also had an education centre, staffed by civilian employees, where both staff and boys were taught to their trade test levels in general education. If you've never been in the army, you'll need some explanation about trade tests.

Leaving school at the age of fifteen, I never took my "advanced" exams. Back in those days if you left school at fifteen, you left with nothing. So I never took my CSE's, 'O' Levels, or 'A' Levels, or GCSE's. I left school with nothing.

When I joined the army, all soldiers needed their trade test qualifications to progress, whether progression was by skill or by promotion. These tests were grouped in three. Yep, that magic number again! A3 to be promoted to L/Cpl, A2 for Cpl and A1 for sergeant and above.

So, in squaddie terms, skills trade tests demonstrated one's skill at killing people; initiative, rifle management, shooting, etc. In the band's terms our skills trade tests were how good you were at initiative, instrument management and playing. Each instrument had its own skills test and these were A3, the lowest skill, A2 and A1. I passed my A3 during my time on boy's service, and my A2 and A1 skills trade tests during my time in the battalion.

Now we can look at promotional, or educational, trade tests. Before any soldier, that's everyone including the band, can be promoted upwards he must have his appropriate general education trade test. I again passed my A3 general education trade test during my time on boy's service, and I was lucky enough to be put on an A2 course during a quiet period in the battalion.

Although these educational trade tests were, by nature, very much military oriented the A1 test was analogous to the GCE 'O' Level exam. I didn't take my A1 general education test until I became an instructor. However, my initiative at getting a place on this course was later to become a bone of contention. More on this later.

Okay, back to what the Depot was all about.

The boy's company, the Junior Parachute Company or JPC, was housed in the same barracks as the adult recruits, although they had separate billets and were never mixed with the adult recruits during their training. The young recruits were given a different training regime until they had passed the recruitment stage and then they were either posted to the JPC's band, JPC's drummers or the JPC's squaddies.

These young soldiers joined at the age of fifteen and were part of JPC until their eighteenth birthday. At that age the squaddies were posted to the Depot recruit company, to undergo intensive soldier training. The bandsmen were posted to their parent battalion band, unless they were sent to Kneller Hall as a pupil first.

Sometimes the young squaddies didn't fancy their future as a fully-fledged soldier but they had a choice; stay in the army and become a fully-fledged soldier or leave the army. What happens if you want to stay in the army but you don't want the rigours of being a squaddie? Well, you joined the band or the drums platoon, usually the band if our DoM had his way. He maintained a good relationship with the rest of the depot instructors and if there was any suggestion that a young chap wasn't up to being a squaddie, he persuaded that chap to join the band.

My job was to teach these young men to cut their mum's apron strings, grow up, learn to read and play music and to ready them for life in the battalions.

When I arrived at the depot it seemed to me that the boys didn't have a structure. All they seemed to do was practise and go to education. Having thought about this I proposed a programme of development for the boys, encompassing general education for their A3 education trade test, music practice and theory for their A3 Skills test, PT for their fitness and drill, with instruments, to hone their marching skills. I also coordinated with the DoM to arrange specific dates for the boys A3 skills tests, to give the boys some time scale to work towards.

I drafted a specific program and put this to the BSM. He sent this upstairs to the DoM for approval, which was granted. During my time as an instructor more boys were sent to the battalion bands having passed their A3 trade tests than at any other time previously.

By way of giving the boys some respite from the rigours of depot life I also coordinated with the battalion BMs to arrange for the boys to integrate with their bands when required. So the boys went out on parades and carnivals. It gave them more confidence and it was an opportunity for them to be part of a bigger organisation and make pals with the "grown-ups". I ensured that the boys were treated with kindness and respect by the grown-ups. It didn't matter if a particular boy couldn't yet play his instrument proficiently, he filled a gap in the ranks that needed filling. If he was a competent player that was a bonus for the BM.

Of particular note was the integration of the whole of the boys' band with the massed bands of the regiment for the Berlin Tattoo. The boys rehearsed with the battalion bands and I accompanied them to Berlin, taking them on organised sightseeing trips at the weekends. We were in Berlin for two weeks and we stayed with 1 Para. This gave me an opportunity to catch up on some gossip... And drinking with my mates.

I also coordinated with the education officer to take the boys out of the depot to give them some "squaddie time". We route marched the full lengths of the Two Moors Walk, taking in Dartmoor and Exmoor, Offa's Dyke on the border of England and Wales, and also The Pennine Way. These exercises gave the boys valuable map reading and orienteering experience.

This period in my army life was the best I had ever known.

I bonded easily with the young musicians, teaching them music theory and practice, and doing everything they did. I sympathised and supported them when they got homesick, and laughed with them on their good days. Each time we had a Depot open day every one of the boys took the trouble to introduce me to his parents who, it must be said, commended the "Changes that they had noticed in their sons, since they had left home," and, "How much they had grown up," and, "How much they respected me."

The battalion BMs all commented that the standard of playing by the boys had improved with each new intake to the battalion bands.

It really meant a lot to me, knowing that I was doing a good job.

My efforts in transforming the young musicians from

boys to men, from learners to competent instrumentalists, from civvies to soldiers, didn't go un-noticed. The DoM promoted me to full corporal. It seemed, at the time, that I couldn't do anything wrong.

Now, the system was that instructors spent two years in the depot and then were posted back to their parent battalion for promotion. Here I was, a full corporal and Depot instructor waiting to be sent to Kneller Hall. I was enjoying Depot life. I was getting on well with my superiors, especially the DoM, and I loved the job that I was doing.

This was my utopia.

I could never, in my wildest dreams, have predicted how my whole world would collapse in on itself because my rogue gene had decided against my present life's path...

CHAPTER 30
Bill's Darkest Days Part 1

Have you ever had that feeling when things are not quite what you expected? Or you know something is wrong but you can't seem to put your finger on it? Have you ever felt that rapid sinking feeling in your stomach when some incomprehensible event suddenly descends on you?

I have.

In the space of about ten days my career was shot to pieces and I never saw it coming in the way it happened.

When I was posted to the depot, in July, 1974, the DoM welcomed me with a chat about my future. In short, he told me that he would recommend me for a place at Kneller Hall (KH) when my tour of duty at the depot had come to an end in two years' time.

There were two intakes per year at KH; one in April and another in September. Looking at the DoM's timescale, it meant that I would be posted to KH in time for the September 1976 intake.

Just two years and a couple of months and my dream of becoming a Bandmaster would be well on track.

It didn't happen.

In 1975 things started to fall apart. Pear shaped, as they say.

I loved my time, and my job, at the depot. I was well

respected and I had persuaded the DoM to tutor me in the art of music arranging. I asked this because I thought that if he could see the standard of my arranging, that, coupled with my trombone playing skills and my teaching skills, he would recommend me for KH without any hesitation.

Everything was going well. My "homework" was inspected by the DoM who returned it to me with a few suggestions to improve my style.

Then I upset him.

I knew that to gain promotion to sergeant and above in the army, one must have passed one's A1 general education trade test. I had already passed my A1 skills trade test when I was in 1 Para, so this was the last hurdle to jump, as far as trade tests were concerned.

I didn't want to bother the DoM with this minor hold-up so I discussed it with the BSM. He endorsed my initiative and, in 1975, I coordinated with the education officer to get me on an appropriate course. A couple of weeks later I was sat in the education centre learning communication skills, world affairs, logistics and man management. I passed, and confirmation of my result was subsequently posted on Pt.1 Orders. This is where things like postings, promotions, exam results and awards were made public. I now had all the trade tests required for posting to KH.

Pt.1 Orders were usually published and displayed last thing every day. The morning after my Pt.1's were displayed I was summoned to the DoM's office, via the BSM. When I asked the BSM why I had been summoned to the DoM's office he merely said, "Don't know. You'd better ask him."

Now this particular response is a typical army reply that usually meant, "I know why, but I'm not going to tell you because you could be in trouble and I don't want to get involved."

I climbed the stairs to the DoM's office thinking, "What can this be about? I surely haven't done anything to upset the boss, have I?"

I tapped on his door and waited for the command "Enter!"

I could tell, straight away, that he was not pleased with something.

"Good morning, sir. The BSM says you want to see me about something," as up-beat as possible.

"Yes. Who gave you permission to go on the A1 education course?"

"Nobody, sir," a puzzled look on my face.

"Well, what gives you the right to jump the queue for education?"

"I... Wasn't aware that I was jumping the queue sir."

"Well, you did. Why didn't you discuss this with me?"

I was now in a tight corner. The DoM's anger at this particular issue was completely unexpected.

"I didn't want to bother you with such a minor issue." This response seemed to enrage him more.

"You call this a minor issue? You've taken up a valuable space on that course. A space that a more deserving NCO could have taken. Who the hell do you think you are? Did you discuss this with anyone?"

Now this observation just didn't sit right. It didn't make sense to me. In a class large enough to accommodate fifteen to twenty places there were just four people on my course. Surely, there was sufficient space to bring in more bodies... If any more bodies had applied for the course!

"I understood that I needed the A1 education trade test

prior to going to KH, so I requested a course."

"So what? Why didn't you ask?"

"I discussed my proposals with both the BSM and the education officer. Both were pleased with my initiative and both gave me permission to attend the course... Sir." I was beginning to feel like I was being knifed in the back for no reason.

"Next time, you don't do things on your own back. You ask me. Is that clear?"

"Yes sir."

"Get out!"

With that I descended the stairs from the DoM's office, my mind in a turmoil. What the hell happened there? I realised one thing, though. I had wounded the DoM's ego, that was for sure!

What I didn't realise at that time was that there was a dark storm brewing on the horizon. A storm I would have no control over. A storm that would fatally damage my future prospects!

I shut myself in my office for a while, mulling over what had happened. But I looked on the bright side and thought that maybe the boss was just having a bad day and he was venting his anger on the nearest person. I decided to put the incident behind me. Tomorrow would be a better day for us both. How wrong can one be?

My arrangements started to attract criticism from the boss. Heavy criticism. "That's all rubbish!" "The boy bandsmen can do better than that!" "Haven't you learned anything?" He was now beginning to hurt my ego. After all, I had managed a score of seventy-one out of a possible pass mark of seventy-five when I took the A.R.C.M., and the boss had previously been pleased with my arrangements. So why the sudden change of heart? I was sure that my arranging skills hadn't deteriorated as badly as he was making out.

Around June time of 1976 I plucked up the courage to ask the boss about KH. My time at the depot was due to expire in July and I was beginning to get a bit nervous about things in general. I had heard nothing about going to the school, and I had heard nothing about returning to 1 Para.

He was a little apologetic. "Oh, yes. I hadn't forgotten. I don't have any application forms at the moment. I'll arrange for you to have an extension to your time in the depot and I'll put you up for the April intake."

Still thinking I was his right-hand man I ask, "Perhaps I can get onto the school and order some for you?"

Angrily, "NO! That's my job. It's none of your business!" With that he walked off. He didn't even wait for a salute, so I didn't give him one.

Inspection of Pt.1's that evening confirmed that I had been granted a one-year extension to my time at the depot.

I carried on with my normal tasks, teaching, drilling, organising postings for the boys that were due to leave JPC. Christmas 1976/77 came and passed. My arrangements still weren't up to scratch. In fact, after Christmas the boss stopped sending them to me.

One morning the BSM and I were chatting while the boys were on PT. He let it slip that a sergeant from 1 Para was coming down to the depot and would be working in the stores until I left. I thought that perhaps the boss was paving the way for me to go to KH.

The sergeant in question was a good pal of mine and I looked forward to meeting him again. When we did eventually meet up he just said, "Watch your back." I asked him what he meant, but he just shook his head negatively.

I thought, "That was a strange off-the-cuff thing to say."

The boss still persisted in needling me over the arrangements. "I've not seen any for a while."

"No sir. You haven't sent any to me for a while."

"You could have asked. And anyway, what's wrong with finding an arrangement of your own?"

"I'll do that right away, sir." I never did.

I was, by now, feeling really jaded. After a period of living in utopia I'm thrown lots of curved balls. Suddenly, I can't do a thing right. I'm criticised for almost everything. I discussed this with the BSM, but he could not come up with any reason why the boss should have turned on me. He just didn't know. Or maybe he did, but he wasn't going to tell me…

The storm that had been brewing on the horizon was getting closer and the sky was getting darker.

Early 1977 arrived and I still had not heard anything about a posting to KH. With my heart in my hands, I took a deep breath and approached the boss when he came down to the band room for a "private discussion" with the BSM. He seemed approachable so I reminded him that I'd not heard anything about the April intake. "Oh!" he says. "There are no vacancies for a trombone. I'll put you up for the September intake." Had he checked? Maybe. Is he pulling my leg? Possible. Is he just delaying the issue? Could be. Is he lying to me? More than likely. But who knows? Certainly not me.

I thought long and hard for a reason why the boss had not applied to have me at the school. Maybe he really was going to put me up for the September intake? Perhaps he doesn't want me to leave, although I kicked that thought into touch in view of the hard time he was presently giving me.

I decided to approach this problem laterally and certainly on the QT. I had a close friend at the school who was in his third year as a student. I telephoned him and asked just one question, "Is there a vacancy for trombones at the school?"

The answer was a definite, "Yes, and where are you. I've been on the school director's back trying to get you up here. They've been waiting for you for ages but my boss says it's your boss's call!"

That clinched it for me.

My boss had no intention of sending me to KH...

CHAPTER 31
Bill's Darkest Days Part 2

 May, 1977, and the time for the April intake to KH had passed, but the boss had told me that he would put me up for the September intake. I was now highly suspicious of his motives. Twice he had made an excuse not to send me to KH, and one of those excuses had proved to be just that… An excuse.

I had to take his latest promise, to send me in September, at face value. In the meantime, I would need yet another extension to my Depot posting. I decided to wait until June to remind the boss, he didn't seem to be too approachable, lately.

The storm brewing on the horizon was now overhead, but it had not yet broken. Was my rogue gene just hovering? Waiting to pounce at the right time to inflict a maximum amount of damage on me? For no apparent reason the hairs on the back of my neck seemed to be perpetually raised, but I had absolutely no idea that the storm was about to break.

Monday, and on arrival at work the BSM called me into his office.

"The DoM wants to see you in his office immediately."

"Okay. What for?"

"Don't know."

I bet he did know.

This time, my climb up the stairs to his office could only be for one of three reasons; he's going to confirm my posting to KH. Unlikely. He's going to confirm my extension for the Depot. Possible. I'm in trouble. Probable. I didn't know why, but it was odds-on favourite that I was going to be faced with a problem. I was wondering what my rogue gene had in store for me this bright, sunny day.

The BSM must have telephoned the boss to say I was on my way up because he was waiting in the corridor just outside his office. He ushered me into his office, his face dark and ominous.

At this juncture I should briefly tell you about my eldest brother. He had a degree in mechanical engineering and had joined the R.E.M.E (Royal Electrical and Mechanical Engineers) at Pirbright, near Aldershot. I visited him a couple of times but I never knew, until this meeting with the boss, that he had left the army. I didn't know when, and I didn't know why.

Anyway, I'm in the boss's office and he is sat on the other side of his desk with tight lips and an accusing look on his face.

The storm breaks!

And rogue gene really gets into his stride with an evil smile on its face.

"What have you been telling your dad?"

"Uh? Nothing sir."

"Don't lie to me. You must have said something to him about you not going to the school."

"No sir. I've not said a word. In fact, I've not even seen

him for over twelve months."

Voices were beginning to be raised.

"YOU MUST HAVE SAID—"

I interrupted him, "I HAVEN'T SAID ANYTHING TO HIM SINCE WE LAST MET!"

"Did you know that your brother has left the army?"

This hit me like a pro boxer's glove. "Urrrm no, I didn't know that. Why?"

"Is that 'why do you ask' or 'Why did he leave'?"

"Why did he leave?"

"He left because he was thrown out for stating a falsehood on his entry form. YOU'RE JUST LIKE YOUR BROTHER, AREN'T YOU?"

"What? No, I'm nothing like him."

"You've just told me you haven't spoken to your dad. That's a lie, isn't it?"

"ABSOLUTELY NOT!"

I decided to step back from this heated argument and lowered my voice, hoping he would do the same.

"Sir… What are you intimating?"

He stared at me for a long time. At least five or six seconds. Then he said, "You don't know about it, do you?"

"Know about what?"

He reached into his drawer and took out a letter. "You'd better read this," he says, throwing the letter at me.

Opening the paper, I immediately recognised Dad's handwriting. I'll not go into the detail of Dad's text, but in brief he had addressed his letter to the Director of Music, Kneller Hall, the head of the army's music and musicians! Equivalent to God! Dad praised my achievements; conducting the local concert band, taking the boys to Berlin, getting promoted. That kind of thing. At the end of his letter, he asked just one question; 'Why hasn't my son been sent to Kneller Hall?'.

My knees went wobbly. My hand started to shake. I felt my stomach bounce off the floor. This is not the kind of thing a twenty-seven-year-old wanted to see, in particular a full Corporal Instructor at the Depot. At the time I cursed both my dad and my rogue gene for putting me in this impossible situation, but looking back I can't really blame Dad for what he did. He was just trying to do his best for me. Having said that, he should have known better. I wasn't some school kid who needed support. I was a grown man, with a wife, and children and responsibilities way above his parental remit.

I placed the letter on the boss's desk, my eyes wide and my face a mix of surprise, anger, puzzlement and devastation. Catastrophic damage had been done by that letter. Damage that I knew, there and then, was irrevocable. I would not be emerging from this storm… Ever!

The boss sits back in his chair and says, "Well?"

"I… I don't know what to say. I didn't…" I was speechless.

"Well, you now have to take an entry exam for KH. Be in the education centre on Wednesday at one p.m. and I'll give you your instructions. Fall out."

I didn't even salute my departure. I didn't think about it. My mind was, again, in utter turmoil. What the hell had my dad done? Why did he feel the need to 'help' me get to KH? With my shoulders drooping and my head hanging low I returned to the band room. The BSM was curious to know what had happened. I told him. The only words of comfort that he offered were, "Well you'd better make sure you pass, hadn't you?"

I knew then that I wasn't going to pass. How could I? My boss had been forwarded a letter from his boss questioning why I had not been sent to KH. My boss didn't have any satisfactory reason for not sending me… Unless I wasn't good enough. But I knew in my own mind that that wasn't true.

On arrival at the education centre, I'm ushered into a classroom full of people. I was horrified. There was a class in progress! I was sat at the back of the class and given an orchestral score to arrange, with some blank manuscript, and told to get on with it, with the parting words, "I'll return in three hours to collect your paper." The boss left and almost immediately the civvy lecturer came down to my desk and apologised that he must continue with his class. It was nigh on impossible to concentrate on my arrangement and listen to 'the geographical influence on the army, navy and air force'.

Three hours later the boss returned to collect my paper.

I went home that night knowing that I was going to fail this entry exam. Astonishingly, many years later I learned from my old bandmaster that I didn't need to take an entry exam. Passage to KH could have been entirely with the boss's backing and endorsement.

On Thursday, the morning after this exam I was again called to the boss's office. He told me that it was no surprise to him that I had failed and that I wasn't good enough for entry to KH. It didn't surprise me, either! He also told me that I was to be posted back to my parent band and that I was to return to 1 Para band on the following Monday.

I was crushed. Despondent. My whole life had just blown up in my face. I resigned myself to hoping I could possibly get an entry to KH in, perhaps, a couple of years' time when things had quietened down. I was wrong again because rogue gene had not yet finished killing my army career!

*

During my time at the Depot the bandmaster that I knew from 1 Para had retired from the army and a new bandmaster had been posted in. The new BM, I knew, had been labelled with a less than complimentary name by the chaps in the band.

At nine a.m. sharp I arrived at 1 Para band room. Now, several of the guys that I left, when I went to the Depot, had either transferred out or had retired. Most of this band was now made up of the boys that I had taught at the Depot. As I entered the band room, I was beckoned by one of these chaps, silently inviting me over with his index finger. As soon as I got close enough he says, "Things have changed here, Bill, since this BM arrived. Stay away from the him. I overheard him telling the DoM that he didn't want you up here."

This didn't come as any surprise to me. If he had been in discussion with the DoM it's probable that a good reason had been given for returning me to 1 Para. Probably that my Depot time had expired. I nodded in acknowledgement and went to introduce myself to the BM.

Coincidentally, he met me in the corridor, just as I was approaching his office.

"Ah, Pollard. Wait in my office. I want a word with you." I didn't go to his office. Instead, I went outside for a cigarette. A few moments later, out of the corner of my eye, I saw the BM return to his office. The BSM was with him. I heard the BM say, "Where is he? I told him to wait in here." Then he bellows, "POLLARD. GET IN HERE NOW!" I didn't. After a few moments, another shout, this time with some anger in his voice, "POLLARD! NOW!" I stubbed my cigarette out and made for the door, meeting the BM mid-way.

"Didn't you hear me calling you? I told you to wait in my office!"

"Oh, I'm sorry, sir. I didn't hear you call me by my rank." There are ways to be disrespectful in a respectful way.

"What?? Who the f*** do you think you are?"

"I'm sure you're aware, sir, that all NCO's are entitled to be called by their rank, no matter who calls them."

"YOU F*****G ARROGANT B*****D! I'LL CALL YOU WHAT I WANT!"

It was at that precise moment that I knew this obnoxious, foul mouthed lout was intent on giving me a hard time. I'd had enough of a hard time from the DoM. I'm damned sure that I wasn't going to let this man with a face resembling a pig bully me.

"Your choice, sir. But I'm sure you've read Queen's Regulations on this matter." This took him a little by surprise.

"I know what the rules are. I don't need to be reminded by you. Look! I know you're a troublemaker. I don't want you making any trouble up here. Okay? If you make any trouble whatsoever, I'll have you round the back!"

Three things here:

1) It's clear that the DoM had fully briefed him on the incident of the letter,

2) He's just violated Queen's Regs by threatening me, and

3) I've had enough of being bullied by people in authority.

As calmly as possible I reply, "Ready when you are, sir. Bring a medic with you 'cos you're going to need one!"

"GET OUT!"

I turn and leave the office. My rogue gene had gone too

far this time. I knew that it was time for me to leave the army.

No, my rogue gene had not won. I was just not going to give it any more room to cause chaos.

I had had enough. This week, some time, I'll go to the company office to request an interview with the company commander with a view to leaving the army.

The BM didn't issue me with a trombone. Instead, I was put on repairing music. No problem to me. I could shut myself in the library and not work to my heart's content.

On Tuesday of that week, the day after my "introduction" to the BM, something happened that was significant in the pattern of things. I didn't realise just how significant until the following day.

At the end of each day orders, in relation to the following day's activities, were given by a senior NCO before the band was dismissed. When the time came for the men to be dismissed, usually about half four in the afternoon, there were no senior NCO's present. I phoned the company office to see if anyone up there had seen them. No. I phoned the drum store. No joy there, either. I phoned the company stores. Nope, not there. It was obvious that the senior NCOs had dismissed themselves for the day without giving any thought to what the rest of the band should do.

Dismissing the band was a big thing. You were sending them home for the day. No more work. No more practice. No more repairing music. Once the band had been dismissed there was no turning back.

I wasn't going to make this decision without making one last attempt at finding a senior NCO. After all, there may be something on the BM's agenda for the following day that the boys in the band should know about. Some order for someone to be somewhere, that kind of thing. The most logical person to find was the BSM, second in command to the BM. So I instructed the band to remain in the band room while I go to the BSM's home to get tomorrow's orders.

Rogue gene saw this as an opportunity to jumble things up a bit.

I went to the BSM's home and was met at the door by his wife. No, she hadn't seen the BSM all day. "Is there a problem?" she asks.

"No, no problem. I just wanted to speak to him about tomorrow's orders."

"Oh? He should be home by now, but I've no idea where he is."

"Perhaps he's in a meeting with the BM."

"Yes, perhaps. I'll let him know you called."

"It's not important. I can see him tomorrow."

I detected a slight tone of animosity in her voice, but as she seemed satisfied that there was no problem, we parted company and I returned to the band room. I dismissed the band with instructions to read tomorrow's Pt.1 Orders and return at eight a.m. to prepare for tomorrow's gig.

The following day, Wednesday, the band was going out on a gig and I was put in charge of the naughty boys because, "That's all you're good for." Still no problem for me. When the coach left the band room, I settled down in the practise room with my friends, the boys I had previously taught in the Depot. I didn't know why they had been classed as "naughty boys", but I guessed that they must have offended the BM in some way. A L/Cpl was in this group and I thought that a bit odd, maybe even eccentric on the BM's part.

The coach arrived back at about four p.m. The naughty

boys were sat in a circle repairing music and passing the time by chatting and joking. We had repaired twenty to thirty scores. The BM struts into the band room from the coach. He had been drinking... A lot.

"What the f***'s going on here?"

I stood and answered, "We're repairing music, sir, as you instructed."

"No, you're not. You're clowning around."

"No, sir. We're just talking."

"BOLLOCKS. You're all f*****g around."

"No, sir. We're repairing music. Would you prefer we sat in silence while repairing music?"

"Don't come it with me Pollard. When I walked in you were laughing and joking. Do you think you're Uncle Remus, or what?"

This comment made the band snigger. I tried, unsuccessfully, not to smile. This enraged the BM.

"Look! You're still f*****g around!"

I said nothing. Still trying to stifle a smile at this ridiculous intercourse I stood there waiting for the BM to spew out more verbal vomit.

"In my office Pollard!"

"Yes sir. Would you mind addressing me by my rank?"

"GET IN MY OFFICE!"

Inside his office I was subjected to more of the BM's abusive tirade. I said nothing. He accused me of being a. "F*****g trouble maker," repetitively. The BSM stood behind him, arms folded. The BM, "Knew you would cause trouble," and threatened to have me "busted". That's demoted in army terms. That didn't bother me because I knew I would be leaving the army. I stood in silence and just looked the BM in the eye, expressionless, and the more I stood in silence the louder and more agitated the BM got.

Suddenly, he ordered L/Cpl {name} into the office. The L/Cpl that had been in the naughty crowd.

"Put Pollard in jail," he ordered.

"What?" the L/Cpl questioned.

"PUT HIM IN JAIL. MARCH HIM TO THE JAILHOUSE!"

I spoke up. "What are you charging me with?"

"You'll find out later. I want you in jail first. Cpl {name}, I'm ordering you to march him up there."

I quietly said, "You realise that you are violating Queen's Regs yet again, sir. You refuse to address me by my rank, you're incarcerating an NCO without charge, you're demanding a rank lower than mine orders me to do your bidding and you have, on numerous occasions, been abusive to a man under your command, namely me." I look at the BSM but get a blank face in return. The BM looked shocked.

I turn to the L/Cpl. "Come on {name}. Let's play the BM's silly game, shall we?"

I ambled through the battalion lines as if I was on a Sunday stroll. The L/Cpl followed the correct protocol by bellowing, in quick time, "LEFT RIGHT LEFT RIGHT LEFT RIGHT LEFT RIGHT," all the way to the guardroom, much to the amusement of the squaddies who had poked their heads out of the billet windows to see what all the noise was about. They cheered me on. I waved back.

At the guardroom the Provost Sergeant asked "What's going on?"

L/Cpl said, "The BM's ordered me to put Cpl Pollard in Jail, sergeant."

"What? What for?"

"Don't know sergeant. He just told me to march Cpl Pollard up here and put him in jail."

The Provost Sergeant looked in my direction. I shrugged my shoulders and held out my hands in a 'don't know' pose. The L/Cpl was dismissed back to the band room.

Provost Sergeant said, "Sit down, Bill. You're making the place look untidy." The Provost Sergeant and I have known each other for years. Certainly, since we had both joined the army. He asks me, "What the f***'s going on?" I told him about everything from the time I had re-joined the battalion. He telephoned the battalion's Adjutant for instructions.

The Adjutant, a lieutenant, came down to the guardroom. We also knew each other from his time in the Depot. "Hello, Bill. What are you doing in here?" I again relayed my side of things. With a look of shock and consternation the Adjutant tells me to go home and report to the battalion 2IC, a major and the band president, at ten a.m. in the morning.

Thursday morning, at ten a.m. precisely, I gently knock on the 2IC's office door and wait for the order, "Come In." Already inside the office was the BM and BSM.

The 2IC opened the conversation by advising me that the BM and BSM had accused me of making trouble and that I had dismissed the band without first obtaining orders.

I was really gutted by this comment. I had also known the BSM since I had joined the army. As privates we had done many things together, had many laughs and we had secrets that only we knew about. At one time we were good friends. I was shocked that he had now turned on me by supporting this poor excuse of a BM. In fact, he was so far up the BM's arse that he could clean his teeth from the inside!

But I was now in another tight corner and I realised that I must put up a fight to keep some semblance of dignity.

2IC said, "Why did you go to the BSM's home?"

It's now obvious that the BSM's wife had bent his ear for not being where he should have been on the evening I called at his house. At the band room? At home? Who knows? At this moment in time, only the BSM knows!

I told the 2IC why I had gone to the BSM's home. The lot. No senior NCO's. No option but to go there.

"What was said to the BSM's wife?"

I told him. The lot. Nothing I had said was considered by me to be derogatory or inflammatory. I added, "What goes on between the BSM and his wife is none of my business." The BSM looked like I had just punched him in the stomach.

2IC said, "What went on when the BM arrived in the band room yesterday?"

I told him. The lot. No punches pulled.

The BM interjects, "He's f****** lying sir. I told you he was a trouble maker."

With that the 2IC stared at the BM, took a deep breath and instructed him and BSM to, "Get about your business." They left the office, barging past me on the way out.

2IC said, "I believe everything you have told me, Bill. I'd like you to let me know anytime and every time the BM is abusive to anyone. Do you mind doing that?"

"No sir."

"Now, you're not going to cause any trouble, are you? You're going to get on with your duties as quietly as possible, aren't you?"

"I'll do everything I can to stay out of trouble, sir, but I can't guarantee that the BM won't put me up before you again.

I can't guarantee anything with regard to this BM."

"I'm aware of that. Just do what you can."

With that he dismissed me.

I didn't go straight back to the band room. I went round the corner to the company commander's office. I had known this guy for many years, also.

I literally hammered on his door, making as much noise as I could. I heard the company commander shout angrily, "WHO THE HELL'S THAT? GET IN HERE!" I opened the door and went to attention in front of him.

"Cpl Pollard? It's not like you to get my attention in this manner."

"No sir, but this is urgent."

"Oh? What's so urgent you have to bang on my door to get attention?"

"I want out of the army, sir, and I want out as soon as possible."

"Sit down. Why the urgency in leaving the army? I thought you were earmarked for KH?"

I told him. I told him about my problems with the Depot DoM, I told him about my abuse since re-joining 1Para, and I told him about the BM's and BSM's apparent efforts to get me discredited and "busted".

I finished my homily with, "I don't want to be in the same army that treats people the way I've been treated."

"That's understandable, son. It's a disgrace that you have been treated like this, but I won't stand in your way."

With that we agreed a date for leaving, we agreed a cost to me for leaving before my contract was up for renewal, we shook hands and he wished me the best of luck for my future. I was now well on my way to leaving the army.

I didn't get any more abuse from the BM. Not that he had any chance to abuse me because I spent the summer in the library not repairing music. Anyway, he never faced me. That was just as well because I was in a good mood to punch his lights out. I heard many years later that he had, at some time during his career, been recalled to KH. This only happens to naughty BM's. Couldn't have happened to a more deserving prat.

The BSM didn't face me either. He couldn't even look me in the eye such was his embarrassment. I think I would have turned his lights off, as well.

November, 1977. Time for me to leave the army for new horizons. I prayed that my rogue gene would let me get on with my life without creating too many problems…

Bill's Epilogue

My dark days were undoubtedly influenced by my rogue gene. That objectionable thing had probably created the final straw that pushed me into leaving the army.

But after the last two chapters I'm going to leave you on a lighter note.

I had been wrestling with the thought of having to leave the army for some time.

Why?

Well, there were two good reasons why I should cut short my army career, but these were probably obscured by my ambition to be a bandmaster.

The first reason was my wife.

Don't get me wrong on this. My wife never, ever, complained about being an army wife, despite the fact that army wives were, in my time, treated by the army as a second thought. She supported me with every decision I made with regard to army life, even though I knew that she didn't like being an army wife. She never complained when we were parted during my unaccompanied postings abroad, particularly my lengthy posting to Cyprus. She had given up a good career to join me in the army and I never thought about this until my latter army years.

However, there's a good example of how army wives were treated.

Wives were expected to attend every NCO mess function that their husbands attended. These were mainly boozy nights, being filled with curry prepared by the army cooks and drinking as much as one could hold, wives included. I knew this wasn't my wife's scene, so I never pressed her to come to a mess "do" with me.

That, in itself, had been noticed by the army. I was once quietly warned, by my boss, that a wife not attending the mess do's indicated a distinct lack of support for me, and that lack of support would hinder my promotional prospects. Like my wife, I considered this to be an outrageous attitude, but I ignored it for the time being.

However, there was an incident during one of my early mess functions that put me off taking my wife to the mess for good.

The night had been its usual booze filled excuse for a good time. One of the squaddie NCOs had collapsed in a drunken heap and he was in everyone's way in the middle of the dance floor, so the blokes pushed him under a table to "sleep it off". His wife was holding her drink a little better than her husband but she was, nonetheless, well and truly brain dead, caused by the excess of vino mixed with almost every type of alcohol that was on show. She had no idea where she was or what she was doing.

With her husband "out of it" the blokes decided to lift this drunken wife onto a table and began chanting "Dance, dance, dance, dance". Not one to refuse such an invitation to be the centre of attention, she started to drunkenly laugh and gyrate to the music. Several of the blokes took it in turn to strip her naked. She was so drunk she even helped to take off her bra and pants, much to all the blokes' delight. The wives just looked on and continued to drink and chat.

With no clothes on she was helped off the table by one of the men and was then carried out to the bar, hotly followed by a few of the others. There are no prizes for guessing what happened next.

That was what made my mind up never to bring my wife to the mess.

The other reason I had thoughts for leaving, was my son.

He was born in 1972, making him five years old when I was having problems at the Depot. He had just started school and I frequently picked him up at going home time. On one occasion I thought I would surprise him. I poked my head into the room where the kids waited to be collected by their parents and saw him sitting a couple of yards away from the door with his back to me. An ideal situation to surprise him, I thought. I was just about to creep into the room when I overheard the conversation he was having with a couple of his friends. There was a lot of bragging going on.

"My dad's a sergeant."

"My dad's a captain."

"My dad drives a Land Rover."

"Well, my dad's got a gun."

That kind of thing.

Young Willy junior had kept quiet throughout this exchange of comparisons until he turned to see me. With pride on his face he pointed, puffed his chest out and said, "That's MY dad!" I felt tears forming in my eyes as I realised that he didn't need to brag about his dad; he was proud of his dad no matter what.

Willy junior started to come home and ask questions like, "My best friend didn't come to school today,", or, "Why is my best friend leaving me?" or, "Why is my best friend upset with me?" He clearly didn't realise that his best friend had been posted away from Aldershot with his dad. In his mind he had done something to upset his best friend and he didn't know what he had done, or how he could repair that friendship.

That hit me hard. My own thoughts drifted to the fact that I hadn't got married to be separated from my wife. Nor had I had children to be separated from them. And anyway, was it fair to keep my son in such an unsettling environment?

So, even before my dark days I had some doubts about staying in the army.

*

Now, throughout one's life communication, as you know, plays an important role. However, my view is that communication with other people is fraught with danger and should be kept tightly locked away until it is absolutely essential that it be used. Don't do it. Do not communicate with anybody unless you have to. I mean it. You will just give your rogue gene something to play with.

Throughout my life my rogue gene has persistently bugged almost every one of my attempts to progress. I recollect a really good quote from someone. Can't remember who or when, but it goes;

"The objective of all dedicated working people should be to analyse thoroughly all situations, anticipate all problems prior to their occurrence, have answers for these problems and move swiftly to solve these problems when called upon. However... when you are up to your neck in alligators it is difficult to remind yourself that your initial objective was to drain the swamp!"

From this you'll gather that despite my good intentions to be communicative, I've spent most of my life fighting alligators.

So, let's explore a few of life's communication problems with what is probably the most functional word in the English language… Shit.

You can smoke shit, buy shit, sell shit, lose shit, find shit, forget shit and tell others to eat shit.

There are lucky shits, dumb shits and crazy shits.

There is bull shit, horse shit and chicken shit.

You can throw shit, sling shit, catch shit, shoot the shit, or duck when the shit hits the fan.

You can give a shit, or don't give a shit and you can find yourself in deep shit or be happier than a pig in shit.

Some days are colder than shit, some days are hotter that shit and some days are just plain shitty.

Some music sounds like shit, things can look like shit and there are times when you feel like shit.

You can have too much shit, not enough shit, the right shit or a lot of weird shit.

You can carry shit, have a mountain of shit or find yourself up shit creek without a paddle.

Sometimes your breath smells like shit.

Sometimes everything you touch turns to shit and at other times you fall into a bucket of shit and come out smelling like roses.

When you stop to consider the facts, the word 'shit' could be the basic building block of the English language. It is a word I have muttered, thought, shouted and used frequently when my life has been manipulated by my rogue gene.

Look at the time I attended my army Resettlement Board.

My Resettlement Board was manned by an army major from the education department, a member of staff from the local employment office and a local trade union rep. I can't remember what union he represented but I do remember my dad advising me that, "You'll not get a job unless you join a union." I was out to prove him wrong, 'cos I did not want to be part of any collective that resembled an army.

Having spent eleven years and ten months as a soldier and musician, what was I going to do for a living out in civvy street? To be honest, I'd had enough of playing the trombone. Anyway, I knew that it was a hard life for a musician out there, unless one is well known or famous, which I wasn't, or one's trombone playing was absolutely the world's best, which it wasn't, or one had contacts to introduce one to somebody with influence, which I didn't. So trombone playing was out.

I thought back to the time before I joined the army, the time I was at school. What lesson did I enjoy doing the most? Not French. Not PT. Not Art... But something creative. Technical drawing. That was the one! Second to music, tech drawing was my next favourite subject. Drawing plans in elevations, Isometric drawings, 3D drawings. That's it! I'll be a draftsman.

Welcomed by three guys at my resettlement board who undoubtedly had a great deal of experience in finding jobs for ex-soldiers, I was optimistic about my future. I was invited to sit. The officer started the ball rolling.

"Good morning, Cpl Pollard. Have you had any thoughts on what you would like to do when you leave the army?"

Be polite. These guys are trying to help. "Good morning gentlemen. Yes sir. I thought about being a draftsman."

The three of them eyed each other and the employment chap wrote something in his notebook. At the start of this interview all three of them made some good, constructive suggestions.

"Have you thought about being in the police force?"

"Thought about it, sir, but I'm looking for a draftsman's job."

"That's interesting work. What about being a fireman?"

"Well, that's certainly an exciting job, sir, but I've decided to be a draftsman."

The three faces were beginning to look contemplative. I'm beginning to think that they just might not be able to come up with anything.

"The ambulance service is looking for people with experience," looking at my file "And I see that you've achieved your A3 medic certification."

"That's correct, sir, but I really do want to be a draftsman". Exasperation creeping in to my tone. Then something dawned on me. What do all these jobs have in common?

Shit! They're all jobs that come with a uniform!

Exasperation creeping into their tone now. The union rep pops in with, "I could get you a placement as a postman."

Maybe I hadn't communicated my wishes accurately enough.

"No thank you. Draftsman."

The union rep again, "I can guarantee you a job as a train driver, or guard."

"Nope. Draftsman!" emphasising the word.

Then the officer comes up with a brilliant idea. "If you're looking for a job with some panache there are several high-end hotels looking for good quality doormen."

Was he serious? Was he taking the piss? That last one took the biscuit! I now decided that they could not help me find a job... Unless, of course, I was willing to wear a uniform. Nope! Had enough of that! Time to move on!

Remind me to strangle my rogue gene should I ever meet it in the flesh.

Addressing the officer I say, "Sir. I've decided that I want to be a draftsman. With the greatest of respect, it doesn't seem that any of you can help me find a job in that line. I'd rather not waste any more of your time and I'm sure you don't wish to waste my time, so perhaps now is a good time to bring this interview to a halt."

"You're right Cpl Pollard. We all wish you the very best of luck for the future."

With that I made my final salute as a soldier and pensively left the building.

I now had about a week left before I became civvy. I packed up all my furniture and transported this to my new home in Worcester Park, Surrey, with the help of the young lads from JPC.

I went round my army quarter repairing holes in the wall where I had hung pictures and a mirror. You were charged thirty pence a hole if there were any visible during your quarter's handover.

I slept on the floor in a sleeping bag. The BM enquired where I was, but nobody knew...

The day before I was due to leave, the band had a KH inspection. This is where the KH DoM inspects the band to make sure it is being managed properly. I was kept out of sight until we performed on the square. The BM didn't want me anywhere near the DoM. After that we had a curry lunch in the band room.

In my last act of defiance, I filled all the pockets of my dress uniform with curry before handing it in, thinking, "This is going to stink the stores to hell, and they'll never guess where that stink is coming from!"

After one last night in my quarters, I was ready to leave the army. I drove back into camp to sign my release papers. I left Aldershot for the last time and on the way to my new life I wondered just how much my rogue gene would influence my future…